Amesha Spentas, Yazatas and Zarathustra
Revelations of a Spiritual Legacy

Nina Vale

Original Title: *Amesha Spentas, Yazatas and Zarathustra: Revelations of a Spiritual Legacy*

Copyright © 2025, published by Luiz Antonio dos Santos ME.
This book is a non-fiction work that explores spiritual concepts and ancient philosophical principles through the lens of Zoroastrianism. With depth and clarity, the author presents a journey into the mystical teachings of Zarathustra, offering spiritual tools and reflections for conscious living, moral clarity, and personal transformation.

First Edition
Production Team
Author: Nina Vale
Editor: Luiz Santos
Cover Design: Studios Booklas / Auren Kael
Consultant: Taren Voss
Researchers: Keela Miren / Doran Hask / Veyra Lint
Layout: Bren Axton

Publishing & Book Identification
Amesha Spentas, Yazatas and Zarathustra: Revelations of a Spiritual Legacy
Booklas, 2025
Categories: Spirituality / Comparative Religion
DDC: **294.5** – CDU: **299.4**

All rights reserved to:
Luiz Antonio dos Santos ME / Booklas
No part of this book may be reproduced, stored in a retrieval system, or transmitted in any form—electronic, mechanical, photocopy, recording, or otherwise—without prior written permission of the copyright holder.

Summary

Systematic Index 5
Prologue 10
Chapter 1   Zoroastrianism 14
Chapter 2   The Life of Zarathustra 20
Chapter 3   The Revelation of Mazda 26
Chapter 4   Ahura Mazda 32
Chapter 5   Names and Titles of Mazda 38
Chapter 6   Angra Mainyu 44
Chapter 7   The Cosmic Conflict 50
Chapter 8   Divine Creation 56
Chapter 9   The Seven Immortals 62
Chapter 10 Vohu Manah 68
Chapter 11 Asha Vahishta 74
Chapter 12 Khshathra Vairya 80
Chapter 13 Spenta Armaiti 85
Chapter 14 Haurvatat 91
Chapter 15 Ameretat 96
Chapter 16 Spiritual Hierarchy 101
Chapter 17 The Yazatas 107
Chapter 18 Mithra, the Judge 113
Chapter 19 Anahita, the Lady of the Waters 118
Chapter 20 Tishtrya, the Starry One 123

Chapter 21 Sraosha, the Guardian of Consciousness 128
Chapter 22 Rashnu, the Weigher 133
Chapter 23 Atar, the Spirit of Fire 138
Chapter 24 Haoma, the Divine Plant 143
Chapter 25 Fravashis, the Protectors 148
Chapter 26 Duality in Spiritual Beings 153
Chapter 27 Invocation Rituals 158
Chapter 28 Feminine Entities 163
Chapter 29 Living Religion 168
Chapter 30 Philosophical Reflection 173
Chapter 31 Unity in Diversity 178
Epilogue 183

Systematic Index

Chapter 1: Zoroastrianism - Introduces the core principles of Zoroastrianism, its ethical dualism between Asha (truth) and Druj (falsehood), and the primary figures Ahura Mazda and Angra Mainyu.

Chapter 2: The Life of Zarathustra - Narrates the life, spiritual journey, revelations, and challenges faced by the prophet Zarathustra, the founder of the faith.

Chapter 3: The Revelation of Mazda - Details Zarathustra's profound visionary experience with Ahura Mazda, establishing free will, the cosmic struggle, and the Amesha Spentas.

Chapter 4: Ahura Mazda - Explores the nature of Ahura Mazda as the supreme, uncreated Lord of Wisdom, the source of all goodness, order, and light in the cosmos.

Chapter 5: Names and Titles of Mazda - Discusses the various names and epithets used for Ahura Mazda, each highlighting a specific aspect of His divine wisdom and creative power.

Chapter 6: Angra Mainyu - Describes Angra Mainyu, the destructive spirit, as the fundamental opponent of Ahura Mazda, representing chaos, falsehood, and corruption.

Chapter 7: The Cosmic Conflict - Examines the ongoing struggle between the forces of good (Ahura Mazda) and evil (Angra Mainyu) across spiritual, cosmic, and human levels.

Chapter 8: Divine Creation - Outlines the seven stages of Ahura Mazda's purposeful creation, associating each stage with an Amesha Spenta and a sacred element.

Chapter 9: The Seven Immortals - Introduces the Amesha Spentas, the seven "Beneficent Immortals," who are direct emanations of Ahura Mazda representing divine qualities and cosmic principles.

Chapter 10: Vohu Manah - Focuses on Vohu Manah, the "Good Mind," the first Amesha Spenta, embodying wisdom, ethical discernment, and compassionate thought.

Chapter 11: Asha Vahishta - Details Asha Vahishta, the "Supreme Truth," representing cosmic order, righteousness, justice, and the purifying power of sacred fire.

Chapter 12: Khshathra Vairya - Explores Khshathra Vairya, the "Ideal Dominion," representing just power, righteous authority, self-mastery, and the integrity symbolized by metal.

Chapter 13: Spenta Armaiti - Discusses Spenta Armaiti, "Loving Devotion," representing humility, piety, patience, reverence, and the sacredness of the Earth.

Chapter 14: Haurvatat - Focuses on Haurvatat, "Wholeness," representing integrity, completeness, health, healing, and the purifying, life-sustaining nature of water.

Chapter 15: Ameretat - Details Ameretat, "Immortality," representing permanence, continuity of life beyond death, resilience, and the guardianship of plant life.

Chapter 16: Spiritual Hierarchy - Explains the structured order of spiritual beings, from Ahura Mazda and the Amesha Spentas to the numerous Yazatas serving cosmic harmony.

Chapter 17: The Yazatas - Introduces the Yazatas, a multitude of spirits "worthy of worship" who protect and govern specific aspects of creation and natural phenomena.

Chapter 18: Mithra, the Judge - Focuses on the important Yazata Mithra, guardian of covenants, sunlight, and justice, who observes promises and judges souls.

Chapter 19: Anahita, the Lady of the Waters - Describes Anahita, the powerful and revered Yazata associated with waters, fertility, purity, and the protection of women.

Chapter 20: Tishtrya, the Starry One - Details Tishtrya, the Yazata associated with the star Sirius and rainfall, who battles the demon of drought to ensure fertility.

Chapter 21: Sraosha, the Guardian of Consciousness - Explores Sraosha, the Yazata of listening, spiritual obedience, and vigilance, who guards human consciousness and guides souls after death.

Chapter 22: Rashnu, the Weigher - Focuses on Rashnu, the Yazata of justice, who impartially weighs the deeds of souls on his scales at the Chinvat Bridge.

Chapter 23: Atar, the Spirit of Fire - Discusses Atar, the sacred spirit embodied in fire, representing truth, purification, and the visible presence of divine light.

Chapter 24: Haoma, the Divine Plant - Describes Haoma, the sacred plant and its associated spirit, used ritually to impart vitality, enlightenment, and longevity.

Chapter 25: Fravashis, the Protectors - Introduces the Fravashis, the immortal higher essences or guardian spirits that accompany and protect individuals, ancestors, and elements of creation.

Chapter 26: Duality in Spiritual Beings - Examines the nuances of duality, including potentially ambiguous aspects of benevolent spirits and the daevas as corrupt counterparts mirroring good entities.

Chapter 27: Invocation Rituals - Details the practice and significance of Zoroastrian invocation rituals, emphasizing purification, the power of sacred words, and the centrality of fire.

Chapter 28: Feminine Entities - Highlights the vital roles of key feminine spiritual figures such as Spenta Armaiti (devotion/earth), Anahita (waters/fertility), and Daena (consciousness/vision).

Chapter 29: Living Religion - Discusses the contemporary practice of Zoroastrianism, showing how its spiritual entities, principles, and rituals remain active and relevant in modern communities.

Chapter 30: Philosophical Reflection - Offers an interpretive view of the Zoroastrian pantheon as an inner, philosophical map of the human soul's journey towards self-knowledge and alignment with divine principles.

Chapter 31: Unity in Diversity - Concludes by emphasizing the underlying unity within the diverse spiritual beings of Zoroastrianism, all reflecting the single light and wisdom of Ahura Mazda.

Prologue

For centuries, the Western gaze was shaped to see the divine through narrow windows. As the centuries passed, what was once sacred mystery became rigid doctrine. Spirituality was converted into a system, and the sacred—which should be as vast as the cosmos and as intimate as the spirit itself—was encapsulated in repeated formulas, catechized, domesticated. The great religious institutions, with their dogmas and power structures, took upon themselves the role of interpreters of the invisible, forgetting that the purest link with the divine never needed intermediaries.

But something began to change. With the dawn of the information age, with free access to previously veiled knowledge, a silent—and profound—movement began. Men and women, restless in their conditioned faith, started to question. To seek. To distrust the stone temples that had replaced the light of consciousness.

And it was in this fertile ground of sacred doubts that a new kind of seeker emerged: one who does not accept ready-made answers, who refuses the comfort of repetition, who yearns for a reunion with what is genuine, ancestral, visceral.

This book is a reflection of that search. It does not offer dogmas—it offers revelations. Revelations of a spirituality born before empires, before crusades, before the need for religious control. Knowledge that was not imposed by swords or political conveniences, but whispered to the soul of a prophet who dared to listen to the voice of the universe in its entirety.

This is not about forgotten myths. It is about wisdom that survived because it remained whole. Because it never needed to adapt to survive. Because its strength lies precisely in its purity.

Zoroastrianism—this spiritual system you are about to explore—does not belong to the past. It belongs to the essence of humanity. The ethics that sustain it, the conscious dualism between truth and falsehood, the clarity of free will as the foundation of life—all this resonates like a familiar echo for those who have allowed themselves to break the invisible chains of domesticated thought.

It is not about believing in a new theology, but about recognizing a knowledge that has always been present, on the margins, waiting for the gaze to become clear enough to see it. The Amesha Spentas, the divine intelligences that structure creation; the Yazatas, spiritual forces that protect the order of the world; Zarathustra, the man who did not found a religion, but rekindled a consciousness. All this is not folklore; it is spiritual code.

This book, with admirable depth, does not deliver canned answers, but leads along a path of understanding that can only be traveled with an open heart and an awakened mind. The modern world tries to fill the spiritual void with self-help formulas or plastic spiritualities, made to entertain, not to transform. Here, the path is different. It is a dive. A return to the roots of a sacred vision of reality where the human being is an agent, not a subject. Where God—Ahura Mazda—does not demand fear, but consciousness. Where good is not imposed by punishment, but conquered by clarity. And where every thought, every word, and every action are instruments of cosmic order or inner ruin.

These are not remote symbolisms, but revelations that dialogue with the most urgent dilemmas of our time: spiritual freedom, ethical integrity, existential meaning. While institutions rush to modernize, to maintain influence, to not lose followers, this ancient wisdom remains serene, offering something that no reform can manufacture: coherence.

It is impossible to go through these pages without being challenged. They confront the passivity of blind faith. They tear down altars built on fear. They dismantle the image of a divine made in the likeness of human authority. In its place, they offer a sacred that breathes with creation, that illuminates from within, that manifests in the daily choice for truth, even when it is silent, unpopular, or difficult.

Prepare yourself to encounter a spirituality that does not ask for conversion, but lucidity. That does not promise easy rewards, but delivers meaning. That does not impose rituals, but reveals eternal principles. This book is a crossing—and like every true crossing, it demands courage. But on the other side lies something that no institutionalized religion has managed to preserve: the recognition that the divine is not a belief, it is a presence. And it is waiting for you in the most sacred space that exists: awakened consciousness.

Yes, this is where the journey begins. Allow yourself to cross this bridge between what you learned and what your spirit always knew. The light that guides this reading does not come from outside. It already burns within you.

Chapter 1
Zoroastrianism

At the heart of the spiritual thought of ancient Persia stood a belief system that would not only influence civilizations for millennia but would shape the essence of the human moral struggle: Zoroastrianism. Unlike the polytheistic traditions that dominated the deserts and plains of Mesopotamia, this faith was consolidated around a rigorous ethical core, sustained by a profound dualism between opposing cosmic forces. It was not a pantheon of gods competing for worship, but a fundamental clash between order and chaos, truth and falsehood, light and darkness—a conflict that resided not only in the heavens but in every human decision.

Zoroastrianism stands as a beacon of moral discipline, where faith is not imposed by ritualistic submission, but by conscious choice. This choice lies between following the path of Asha—truth, order, righteousness—or falling into the domains of Druj—falsehood, deceit, deviation. Existence, in this sense, is a battlefield where every thought, word, and action weighs on the cosmic scale.

This concept is not limited to the abstract plane; it is deeply experiential. Every human being is invited, almost urged, to participate in this invisible war that moves the universe.

Ahura Mazda, the Lord of Wisdom, is the radiating center of this doctrine. Not a deity molded in form or idols, but a creative consciousness, the very ordering intelligence of the cosmos. He is infinite light, not in the literal sense, but as a living metaphor for knowledge, wisdom, moral clarity. His existence is not made known through visible appearances, but in every instance of creation that sustains life, in the harmony of the elements, in the justice that governs destinies, in the consciousness that awakens in human hearts. He is not a distant god; He is immanent in the order that protects the world from dissolution.

In radical opposition to this benign presence is Angra Mainyu—the Spirit of Destruction. Not a being with claws or horns, but the essence of chaos, the negation of creation, the darkness that wishes to extinguish the spark of life and truth lit by Ahura Mazda. Angra Mainyu creates nothing; he corrupts. He does not form; he dissolves. His existence is not complementary to Mazda's, but a continuous assault on the integrity of reality. He is a force that contaminates, not one that builds; that obscures, not one that reveals.

The tension between these two principles—Spenta Mainyu, the Holy Spirit of Mazda, and Angra Mainyu—structures the cosmos in layers of moral significance. There is no neutrality in this world. What exists is either part of the sacred creation or part of the plan of destruction. Ethics, therefore, becomes an existential imperative. It is not possible to truly exist without taking a stance.

This principle reverberates in the doctrine's best-known formula: "Good thoughts, good words, good deeds." These three pillars are like keys that connect the individual to the flow of light emanating from Ahura Mazda. To deviate from them is to allow the shadow to expand.

The revelation of this cosmology was neither random nor the fruit of collective meditation. It was communicated to one man: Zarathustra. A prophet born in a time of spiritual instability, where multiple gods and bloody rituals consumed the people's faith. He emerges as a spiritual insurgent, breaking with idolatry and declaring that there is only one deity worthy of worship. His voice announces a theological revolution: there are no gods fighting for offerings; there is a single source of good, whose existence calls for responsibility, not fear. By proclaiming Ahura Mazda as the Sole Creator, Zarathustra not only breaks with polytheism but inaugurates a new concept of faith—one born of consciousness, not custom.

The writings attributed to Zarathustra are gathered in the Gathas, hymns that not only outline religious precepts but vibrate with mystical poetry. In them, one can perceive the density of the relationship between the divine and the human. Ahura Mazda does not demand submission, but cooperation. He does not reign by terror, but by wisdom. He reveals, He does not impose. And upon being revealed, the world gains meaning. Ethics, nature, time, destiny—everything intertwines in the luminous web that Mazda weaves with those who choose Asha.

This revelation unfolds in the existence of the Amesha Spentas—spiritual beings who are not gods themselves, but aspects of divinity itself. They represent not just ideas or virtues, but real categories of creation. The Good Mind, the Supreme Truth, Loving Devotion—these are not abstractions; they are active intelligences, conscious forces that sustain the world. They do not compete among themselves, for all are manifestations of the same principle: the ordering wisdom. Each of these beings will be revealed clearly in the following chapters, but it is essential to understand here that Zoroastrianism is not a disguised polytheism. It is a spirituality where the multiplicity of forms expresses essential unity.

Time also possesses a moral structure within this worldview. The universe was created with purpose, in stages, and follows a timeline with a beginning, middle, and end. It is not cyclical like in other Eastern traditions. It is linear and teleological. The world moves towards total renewal, the Frashokereti. In this glorious end, evil will be annihilated, time will be purified, and all the dead will resurrect for a final judgment, where each soul will cross the Chinvat Bridge—a subtle passage that widens for the righteous and narrows like a blade for the wicked. This judgment is not arbitrary but a direct consequence of the life lived.

Fire occupies a central role in religious practice. Not out of elemental fetishism, but because it is the visible manifestation of divine light. In every temple, a flame is kept burning as a sign of Ahura Mazda's presence, of the moral clarity that one wishes to maintain. Fire is the link between worlds, between the materiality of life and the purity of spirit. To look at the fire, protect it, pray before it—is like gazing into the essence of the divine itself. Zoroastrian prayer, thus, is not passive murmuring, but an active affirmation of connection with the good.

Despite losing its dominant position after the Islamization of Persia, Zoroastrianism survived in the hearts of those who migrated to India—the Parsis—and those who remained in Iran as silent guardians of an ancient faith. Its doctrines echoed in other religious traditions: the ideas of heaven and hell, final judgment, messianism, and even the figure of the devil are distant echoes of Zoroastrian theology. Even today, its truths resonate in the mysteries of human choice, in the invisible war waged within each person.

By preserving a millennial tradition of individual responsibility and moral clarity, Zoroastrianism invites human beings to become not just spectators, but active agents in the drama of the universe. This call to ethical action, sustained by trust in the human capacity to consciously choose good, breaks with the idea of a passive and resigned spirituality. It is not about escaping the world, but inhabiting it with lucidity, like someone walking through shadows holding a torch. The sacred fire, far from being a simple symbol, becomes a living mission: to keep the flame of righteousness burning against the contrary winds of chaos.

This system of thought not only answers the existential concerns of its time but anticipates questions that still permeate us today—moral responsibility, free will, the nature of evil, and the possibility of redemption. The strength of the Zoroastrian doctrine lies precisely in its ethical depth and its appeal to awakened consciousness, a timeless invitation for every human being to recognize the power they hold over the course of their own soul. By recognizing that every act resonates in the fabric of reality, it offers the believer an internal compass, firm and luminous, even in the darkest moments.

In this way, Zoroastrianism remains a living legacy, not because it survived intact through time, but because it left deep marks on the spiritual imagination of humanity. Its prophet, its ethics, and its vision of destiny are, to this day, mirrors in which one can glimpse the highest of human yearning for meaning. And as long as there are those who, faced with darkness, choose the flame, the voice of Zarathustra will continue to echo, like a call to the courage of living righteously.

Chapter 2
The Life of Zarathustra

In a land bathed by arid horizons and vast silences, a man was born who would alter the course of human spirituality. Zarathustra, also known as Zoroaster, did not emerge from the bosom of political power, nor from the priestly castes that dominated the cults of the time. He appeared as a stranger among his own, bearer of a gaze that saw beyond the smoke of sacrifices and the clamor of warrior gods. His presence in the world marked the eruption of a new consciousness, and his path would be defined not by ambition, but by a revelation.

Zarathustra lived, according to scholars, between 1500 BC and 600 BC, although precise dates remain shrouded in temporal mists. He was likely born in the region of Bactria or Media, where polytheistic practices dominated religious rituals. The world into which he first breathed was marked by bloody offerings, multiple deities, and a priestly aristocracy that kept spiritual power under hermetic control. There was no room for questioning. The gods demanded blood, men obeyed, and the cycle repeated under the promise of divine protection and abundant harvests.

Zarathustra, however, was a man of intense interiority. From a young age, he refused to accept the prevailing dogmas without confronting them with his mind. He saw, in the shedding of animal blood, a dissonance with what he felt was sacred. Spirituality, for him, should emanate from wisdom, compassion, moral order—not from fear, not from bargaining, not from blind sacrifice. This inner discomfort grew like an ember under his skin, until it became a voice. And this voice, one day, spoke to him definitively.

Tradition tells that at the age of thirty, Zarathustra retreated to the banks of a sacred river, surrounded by mountains and silence. There, in retreat and contemplation, he received the vision that would change everything: Ahura Mazda revealed Himself to him. But this revelation did not come in thunder or flaming mirages. It came as absolute understanding, as light that dissolves all shadows. Ahura Mazda, the Lord of Wisdom, presented Himself as the only true divinity, source of all good, of all just creation. Beside Him were the Amesha Spentas, manifestations of His own essence, companions in the cosmic mission. And opposing them, the negation: Angra Mainyu, the destroyer.

Zarathustra understood, in that instant, that the universe was the stage of a moral drama. Good and evil were not complementary forces, but opposed in essence. The human being, with mind and freedom, was called to participate in this conflict. Not by the sword, but by conscious choice. With this mission engraved on his soul, he returned to the world of men.

But the return was not triumphant. His teachings were received with suspicion, mockery, and hostility. The old priestly caste saw his words as a threat to the established order. The ethical monotheism he preached shook the foundations of the prevailing spiritual authority. He spoke of a single God who did not accept blood sacrifices but called for inner purity. He proclaimed that each person was responsible for their soul and their role in creation. This doctrine was unbearable for a system based on hierarchies and submissions.

Zarathustra was forced into exile. He wandered for years among tribes and villages, sowing words wherever he found minimally open ears. In his journey, he had continuous visions that strengthened him, experiences with spiritual beings that broadened his understanding of the cosmos. Among them, the most striking was Vohu Manah, the "Good Mind," who led him into the presence of Ahura Mazda in the first revelation. This spirit became his constant guide, showing him that truth must be sought with a clear mind and a heart free of hatred.

Zarathustra's fortunes changed when he arrived at the court of King Vishtaspa, a ruler with a more open mind and a restless spirit. After hearing the prophet's teachings, Vishtaspa converted to the new faith and became his protector. This moment marked the beginning of the real spread of Zoroastrianism. With the support of political authority, the teachings could expand, hymns were recited freely, and the principles of the new religion began to shape a civilization.

Even with this support, Zarathustra never let himself be seduced by power. He did not found luxurious temples nor create a privileged caste. His life remained simple, focused on teaching, listening to the needy, and cultivating the sacred word. He wrote—or inspired the writing of—the Gathas, the lyrical compositions that condense his theology. In these verses, he speaks of the judgment of souls, the bridge leading to the afterlife, the final renewal of the world. But he also speaks of daily choice, constant effort, the slow and profound victory of truth over falsehood.

Zarathustra died as he lived: shrouded in mystery. Some traditions say he was murdered by fanatics, others that he disappeared silently into the desert. The fact is that his legacy traversed the ages. His doctrine would be the basis for empires, inspiration for mystics, reference for philosophers. But his greatness does not lie in temporal achievements. It lies in the lucidity he imprinted upon the role of consciousness. He was the first to declare that the human being is free, and that this freedom is sacred, for it is the weapon with which one confronts evil.

There is no way to understand the spiritual pantheon of Zoroastrianism without going through the life of its founder. For Zarathustra not only preached the existence of Ahura Mazda—he lived this faith with rare wholeness. His spiritual journey was made of loss, desert, persecution, ecstasy, and absolute fidelity to what he saw. He was not afraid to break with centuries of tradition. He did not retreat in the face of solitude. In his voice, the world heard for the first time that good is not a dogma, but a choice. And that this choice is the light that breaks any darkness.

The life of Zarathustra is a living testimony that truth is not imposed by force, but by coherence between word and action. He was not just a messenger of doctrines, but the very embodiment of what he preached. His path, made of exile and revelation, shows that genuine spirituality often walks on the margins of power and convenience. By refusing empty rituals and hierarchical systems that imprisoned the sacred in fixed formulas, Zarathustra freed faith from superstition and led it back to the field of consciousness—where every human being is called to be a priest unto themselves.

His message continues to echo because it touches an essential point of existence: the freedom to choose good even when everything around seems to lean otherwise. Zarathustra did not promise automatic protection, nor divine favors in exchange for rites. He offered responsibility. Each person, upon awakening to the presence of Ahura Mazda, took upon themselves the duty to sustain order against the advance of chaos, not with violence, but with righteousness. This sense of personal mission, grounded in an ethics of discernment, shaped a type of religiosity that does not need opulent temples, but attentive hearts and vigilant minds.

Thus, Zarathustra's journey remains relevant not because it belongs to the past, but because it illuminates the present with its serene flame. In a world increasingly saturated with noisy dogmas and instant truths, his life reminds us that true revelation requires silence, courage, and fidelity to what is understood as just. He did not leave us just a religion, but a way of being in the world with dignity and clarity—like one who, even amidst darkness, walks certain that light is not just a destination, but a path chosen at every step.

Chapter 3
The Revelation of Mazda

The night was thick as the doubt that plagues the soul before the dawn of understanding. On the bank of a sacred river, surrounded by the solitude of nameless mountains, Zarathustra experienced what could never be contained by human words. There, where the sounds of the world fell silent, and only the pulse of the invisible echoed in his bones, the revelation occurred: not through thunder or fiery apparitions, but as a clarity that dissolves all veils. The presence of Ahura Mazda did not impose itself—it revealed itself.

There was no imposition. There was no fear. There was recognition. Zarathustra did not see a god molded in the image of human passions, thirsty for offerings or vengeance. He did not hear promises of power nor demands for dominion. What was revealed to him was something much deeper: Ahura Mazda, the cosmic intelligence, was not a being seeking to be worshiped. He was the very order that sustains reality, the wisdom that permeates all that is pure, the light that illuminates not the eyes, but the mind. That moment was not just the beginning of a religion—it was the establishment of a new understanding of existence.

Ahura Mazda spoke. But His words were not sounds vibrating in the air; they were truths vibrating in consciousness. The first of these was the most devastating: man is free. There is no fixed destiny. There are no cosmic forces imprisoning the soul in cycles of error. There is choice. And this choice is sacred. The human being, with a rational mind and a sensitive heart, is solely responsible for their own path. Nothing is imposed. Truth must be accepted by conviction, not coercion. Free will is, in Zoroastrianism, the greatest gift and the most severe responsibility.

Zarathustra understood, then, that the world is sustained by a moral principle. Reality is not neutral. Ahura Mazda's creation is pure, harmonious, luminous. But this creation is under constant attack. Angra Mainyu, the destructive spirit, is not a creature of Mazda, but a presence that chose the opposite path: that of falsehood, corruption, chaos. He has no substance of his own; he lives by corrupting what has been created. He is the rot that needs the fruit to exist. This revelation was not symbolic; it was literal. Zarathustra saw with the eyes of the soul that the universe is at war—and that humans are not mere spectators, but warriors.

The revelation continued. Ahura Mazda does not act alone. He manifests through seven divine aspects, called the Amesha Spentas—"Beneficent Immortals." They are not separate beings, but forms through which the supreme wisdom acts in the world. Each embodies a sacred quality, an active virtue expressed both in creation and within the human being. The "Good Mind" leads to discernment and compassion. The "Supreme

Righteousness" maintains order in the cosmos. "Loving Devotion" roots faith in the earth. And so on. The revelation of Mazda was not a divine hierarchy—it was an architecture of light.

Each of these aspects corresponds to elements of existence: the sky, water, fire, metals, animals, the earth, humanity itself. Everything that exists has a purpose and carries within it a spark of creative wisdom. The material world is not illusory or cursed—it is sacred. Creation is good. The problem does not lie in the body, the earth, or desire. It lies in the wrong choice, the twisted thought, the action that breaks order. With this, Zarathustra broke with centuries of spiritual thought that despised the physical world. He did not ask for escape from the world. He asked for transformation.

This revelation gave rise to the threefold commandment that would become the heart of Zoroastrianism: Humata (good thoughts), Hukhta (good words), Hvarshta (good deeds). They are not just ethical precepts. They are spiritual keys. To think well is to align oneself with Vohu Manah. To speak well is to manifest Asha Vahishta. To act well is to participate in Mazda's cosmic effort. These acts are not merely social or moral—they have metaphysical repercussions. Every good choice is a victory over Angra Mainyu. Every just gesture is a ray of light that weakens the darkness.

Truth, for Zarathustra, is not the property of a spiritual elite. It is accessible to all who purify their inner selves. Ahura Mazda does not speak only to priests—He speaks to all who have a clean mind and a sincere heart. Therefore, revelation does not come through secret rituals or hidden languages. It manifests in light, in reason, in justice. The religion revealed by Mazda is a religion of clarity, not mystery. That is why fire—a symbol of visible truth—becomes the center of Zoroastrian rituals.

During the revelation, Zarathustra was not just instructed. He was transformed. His mind opened as if layers of dust were removed. His spiritual vision began to see clearly what was previously blurred. He understood that his mission was not to found a new caste or a new religious empire. It was to be the voice of choice. He was to announce to the world that the path of light is available, but it is narrow and requires effort. That there is no automatic salvation, nor inherited redemption. That each soul is measured by its own righteousness.

This revelation did not end with words. It became action. Zarathustra began to live what he saw. He did not teach what he did not practice. He did not proclaim what was not evident in his way of walking, listening, deciding. Wherever he went, his presence was a silent call to integrity. Many hated him, for truth disturbs. Many feared him, for freedom frightens. But some listened to him—and with that, the light spread.

The message revealed by Mazda did not demand golden temples. It demanded a lucid mind and a righteous life. Rituals should be simple, yet profound. Words should be weighed on the scale of consciousness. Actions, measured by universal justice. This revelation demanded discipline, but offered something unique: meaning. There was no more chaos, no chance.

Everything was part of a plan, and every being was a living piece of the cosmic harmony.

Zarathustra never claimed divinity for himself. He never accepted being worshiped. His greatness resided precisely in this: he knew he was only the bearer of the message, not its origin. Everything came from Ahura Mazda. The revelation was alive, and every person could access it, provided they cultivated inner truth. This was the greatest spiritual revolution of his journey: restoring to human beings the right to dialogue with the divine without ambitious intermediaries.

In the revelation of Mazda, Zarathustra found the map of the cosmos, but also the mirror of the soul. He discovered that the universe pulses in duality, but that this struggle is not eternal. Good will win. Creation will be restored. Evil will be overcome not by force, but by the persistence of light. And every man and woman is called to participate in this outcome. There is no room for spectators. Revelation is not a dogma to be memorized, but a call to be lived.

The revelation Zarathustra received did not intend to found a closed system of beliefs, but to open the world to the possibility of a new kind of consciousness—an awakened, responsible consciousness committed to the construction of good. The cosmos, far from being a stage of immutable destiny or arbitrary divine will, was presented as a morally accessible reality, moldable by human action. In this horizon, the sacred is not confined to an unreachable beyond, but inhabits the everyday, the silent choice, the sincere gesture, the clean thought.

The doctrine revealed by Mazda does not compel us to fear—it invites us to understand. By recognizing free will as the center of existence, the revelation dissolved fatalism and established a new covenant between the human and the divine. It is not about collective or predestined salvation, but about intimate redemption, achieved step by step, thought by thought. Each soul carries within itself not only the weight of its decisions but also the nobility of its potential. This gives Zoroastrianism a profoundly hopeful dimension, where good is not a privilege of a few enlightened ones, but a universal possibility.

The struggle between light and darkness ceases to be a distant mythical clash and reveals itself as an internal tension, present in the breath of each day. Therefore, the revelation of Mazda remains perennial: because it speaks not of a past fixed in stone, but of a continuous journey. The sacred word is not confined to scriptures but lives in the decisions of those who choose Asha. The world still pulses with the invitation made to Zarathustra: recognize the light, act with righteousness, and refuse to compromise with chaos. This is not just the essence of a faith—it is the affirmation that every life matters, every choice resonates, and every soul can become, by its own will, an extension of the light that orders the universe.

Chapter 4
Ahura Mazda

The vastness of the sky, when yet unscarred by human presence, reveals the silent architecture of creation. The brilliance of the stars, the rhythm of the winds, the precision with which natural cycles repeat—all point to an intelligence that not only originated the cosmos but sustains it with purpose and clarity. This intelligence, according to Zarathustra, has a name: Ahura Mazda. He is not an entity forged in the image of humans. He has no face, dwells not in temples, demands no sacrifices. Ahura Mazda is the very wisdom that permeates reality.

Ahura means "Lord," and *Mazda*, "Wisdom"—but these translations do not capture the totality of what He represents. More than a superior being, Ahura Mazda is the conscious manifestation of light, order, and truth. His essence is as vast as the universe itself, and His presence reveals itself not through imposition, but through recognition. Where there is harmony, there are traces of Him. Where there is justice, His hand is visible. Where there is clarity of thought and goodness in action, His voice still whispers.

He possesses no physical form, and precisely because of this, He cannot be represented. Any image attempting to capture Him would be a betrayal of His essence. Ahura Mazda transcends matter, not by rejecting it, but by being its origin and purpose. All that is good, true, and pure emanates from Him as a reflection of a light that never extinguishes. Unlike other ancient deities, He has no genealogy, was not born of another being, did not emerge from primordial chaos. He is eternal, without beginning or end. And yet, He is present in every leaf, every breath, every impulse of justice.

When creating the world, Ahura Mazda did not do so out of necessity or amusement. He created it out of love for order. Each element of creation was shaped with intention: the sky to protect, the water to purify, the fire to illuminate, the earth to sustain. Nothing was done by chance. Every part of the universe carries a spiritual function. The world, for Him, is both temple and work. It does not demand servile worship, but conscious cooperation. He does not desire subjects, but allies.

To maintain this creation, Ahura Mazda emanates seven divine intelligences—the Amesha Spentas—who act as extensions of His will. They are not independent, possess no ego, do not rival each other. Each represents an aspect of Mazda Himself. Vohu Manah, the Good Mind, guides humans to discernment. Asha Vahishta, the Supreme Truth, sustains order. Spenta Armaiti, Loving Devotion, roots faith in the earth. Khshathra Vairya, the Ideal Dominion, regulates power with justice. Haurvatat and Ameretat, Wholeness and Immortality, preserve the integrity of creation. It is these aspects that reveal, in fragments, who Ahura Mazda is.

But He goes beyond His attributes. He is total consciousness. He knows all that was, is, and will be. Not by spying or controlling, but because all existence vibrates in His wisdom. His knowledge is not static; it is alive. He understands human paths, knows the dilemmas, comprehends the weaknesses. But He never forces a choice. His greatness lies precisely in the freedom He grants. Each soul is free to follow Him or not. And this freedom is the thread that weaves Zoroastrian morality: following Ahura Mazda is an ethical choice, not a mystical imposition.

There is no shadow or ambivalence in His nature. He is pure. He is the complete absence of evil, for evil does not originate from Him. Angra Mainyu, His opposite, is not His brother, nor His creation. He emerged from his own decision to deny the truth. Ahura Mazda did not create him but confronted him. And His fight is not waged with armies, but with light. Every time a creature chooses truth, it weakens Angra Mainyu. Every good deed is a spark of Mazda lit in the world.

Ahura Mazda reveals Himself in the mind and spirit. He does not impose Himself like thunder but illuminates like dawn. Therefore, Zoroastrianism has always privileged thought: true faith is born from awakened reason, not blind obedience. The man who thinks righteously, speaks sincerely, and acts justly already lives in communion with Ahura Mazda, even without knowing Him by name. He is present where good flourishes, where evil is fought firmly, and where the dignity of being is preserved.

His faithful should not bow in fear but walk upright with responsibility. Ahura Mazda does not desire empty worship, but just actions. His religion is practical, everyday, committed. The spirituality He inspires does not hide in caves but expresses itself in common life: in the honesty of work, in the protection of the vulnerable, in the care for the elements of nature. The world is the altar where His name is honored, and every righteous gesture is a prayer.

The absence of image does not make Ahura Mazda abstract—it makes Him intimate. He is not outside; He is within. In every ethical choice, in every renunciation of selfishness, He shines. His temple is the heart of the just, and His true worship is righteousness. There is no need for intermediaries, for He communicates directly with those who purify themselves through effort. Prayer, to be heard, need not be long or ceremonial. It just needs to be sincere. The light of Ahura Mazda penetrates the silence and responds to the soul with peace.

Ahura Mazda is the God who invites, not obliges. He guides but does not manipulate. He observes but does not punish arbitrarily. His justice is measured by the balance of being itself. At the end of time, when Angra Mainyu is defeated and the world renewed, each soul will be judged not by dogmas or rituals, but by its fidelity to truth. The fire of consciousness, which always burned within, will be the light of that judgment. And those who chose Mazda will see that, even in the darkest nights, He was always by their side—not as a superhuman figure, but as the subtle voice calling to righteousness.

In the vastness of His silence, Ahura Mazda continues to be the inexhaustible source of the order that structures the world and the clarity that illuminates the human mind. He does not demand idolatry nor presents Himself as an impenetrable enigma; His mystery lies precisely in the transparency of His presence, in the sharpness of His ethics. His divinity is not imposed as a burden, but as a direction, a moral compass always pointing towards the north of truth.

At the center of the Zoroastrian religious experience, therefore, lies not fear, but dignity: the human being is treated as capable, conscious, worthy of participating in the divine project of maintaining cosmic harmony. Ahura Mazda does not propose a faith confined to the supernatural, but a spirituality integrated into reality. His voice echoes in the structures of the world, but also in the inner silences that precede the right choice.

By becoming the supreme reference of wisdom, He shifts the axis of religion from superstition to consciousness, from submission to lucidity. It is not raw power that defines His rule, but coherence with the good. This characteristic makes His figure one of the most revolutionary in ancient religious thought: He does not need to be feared to be followed; He needs only to be understood to be loved.

Following Ahura Mazda is, therefore, more than an act of faith—it is a commitment to justice, clarity, integrity. It is not about pleasing a superior being, but about responding to the call of one's own awakened consciousness. In this serene invitation, Mazda offers human beings a noble role: that of co-creator of order in the world. And it is in this role that true worship is found, not in opulent rituals, but in the simplicity of the correct choice, repeated every day, like someone lighting a flame—not to be seen, but to keep the light alive within the night.

Chapter 5
Names and Titles of Mazda

Ahura Mazda does not hide behind masks nor needs veils to preserve His mystery. He is, by essence, constant revelation. However, His presence is so vast, so absolute, that a single word could not contain Him. Therefore, over the centuries, those who bowed before the universal wisdom manifested in this supreme Being gave Him many names, titles, and epithets. Each of these is a human attempt to touch the ineffable, to describe, albeit in fragments, the magnitude of the source of all light, order, and truth.

These names and titles are not poetic adornments. They are spiritual tools, keys that open dimensions of the sacred and guide the human mind towards clarity. With each name invoked, one does not call upon a distinct deity, but illuminates an aspect of Ahura Mazda's total presence. Just as white light unfolds into infinite colors when passing through a crystal, the unified nature of Mazda manifests in multiple forms of wisdom.

"Lord of Truth" is perhaps the oldest and most fundamental among His titles. Truth, in Zoroastrianism, is not just logical correctness or fidelity to facts. Truth is the very fabric of reality, the invisible structure that keeps the cosmos in balance. By naming Him "Lord of Truth," the faithful acknowledge that Ahura Mazda does not merely teach what is true—He *is* Truth. His essence vibrates in every well-ordered atom, in every cycle that runs its course with justice. Before Him, falsehood cannot stand. Falsehood dissolves like shadow before the sun.

"Creator of Light" is another title that resonates strongly in Zoroastrian hearts. Light, in this context, is not just a physical phenomenon, but a spiritual reality. It symbolizes knowledge, clarity, the presence of good. To invoke Mazda as the creator of light is to recognize that all wisdom that dispels fear, all discernment that guides consciousness, all justice done in the name of compassion, emanates from Him. The light that man seeks outside shines first within, when aligned with cosmic order.

"Supreme Wisdom" is perhaps the name that best synthesizes the heart of the Mazdaean doctrine. The word "Mazda" already means wisdom, but by emphasizing it as supreme, the ancient texts make it clear that this is not practical or technical intelligence. It is wisdom that surpasses the limits of logic and sensory experience. It is the consciousness that knows the end from the beginning, that guides without forcing, that loves without subjugating. This wisdom is creative because it is just, and it is just because it knows all causes and effects before they manifest. It is this wisdom that sustains the ethics of Zoroastrianism: to act with wisdom is to act with Mazda.

There are also titles like "Father of the Amesha Spentas," which reveals His role as the origin of the seven divine spirits governing creation. Each of these beings represents a divine quality: the clear mind, truth, devotion, just dominion, wholeness, immortality, and existence itself. By calling Him Father, one speaks not of fatherhood in the human sense, but of the original source—all that is good, useful, ordered, and virtuous is born from Him. He is the root that nourishes the branches of the cosmos.

Another name carrying deep spiritual weight is "He Who Hears Thoughts." In Zoroastrianism, there is no room for ritual deceit. What counts is the true intention, the quality of thought even before the word is spoken. Ahura Mazda is attentive to the mind, not out of punitive surveillance, but because it is there that moral choice is born. He knows the weight of silences, doubts, unexpressed desires. The judgment, when it comes, will not be based on appearances, but on the hidden truth of thoughts.

In some texts, He is also called "Lord of Cosmic Order." This refers to the concept of Asha—the order that permeates all that is just, pure, and true. Asha is not a simple moral or natural code; it is the very manifestation of Ahura Mazda in the world. To name Him Lord of Order is to confess that the universe is not chaotic, that there is structure, symmetry, direction. The chaos observed is not His work, but the result of the action of Angra Mainyu, the spirit of falsehood and confusion.

There are names reflecting His relationship with human beings. "Guardian of Just Souls" is one of these. He does not abandon those who choose righteousness. He stands beside them in every invisible battle, inspiring courage, clarity, and compassion. Throughout life, His presence may seem discreet, but at the moment of crossing into the beyond, He reveals Himself as judge, guide, and protector. His justice is serene but infallible. He does not condemn for error but rewards sincerity. His balance does not weigh words; it weighs integrity.

Each of these titles is also an invocation. By saying them in prayer, the faithful aligns themselves with the vibration they evoke. By calling Him Supreme Wisdom, the worshiper seeks clarity. By calling Him Creator of Light, they ask for discernment. By naming Him Lord of Truth, they invoke courage to remain whole. Thus, the names of Mazda are not just forms of reverence. They are paths. They are invocations that transform the inner self. They are living memories of the covenant between man and the divine.

The recitation of these names is part of Zoroastrian rituals. In daily prayers, at sunrise and sunset, the faithful murmur them before the fire, the visible symbol of divine presence. The fire is not worshiped but revered as the purest representation of spiritual light. By pronouncing the titles of Mazda before the flame, the worshiper acknowledges that what is invisible can be touched by the spirit if the mind is clear and the heart, clean.

Ahura Mazda is not reduced to any of these names. All of them together would still be insufficient to contain His greatness. But by spreading them throughout the world like seeds of light, Zarathustra and his successors offered man ways to approach the ungraspable. The names, thus, do not imprison. They liberate. They invite. They remind that although the absolute cannot fit into words, it is possible to live it in thought, word, and action.

The relationship between the faithful and Ahura Mazda is shaped by these titles. They teach to see Him not as a cosmic tyrant, but as a compassionate master. Not as an implacable judge, but as a silent guide. The names reveal that the divine is not distant. It is present. It is in everything that is good, everything that is just, everything that is true. It is in the word that consoles, the gesture that protects, the decision that honors. To know the names of Mazda is, ultimately, to know oneself in one's purest state.

Each title bestowed upon Ahura Mazda reveals not only attributes of the divine but also deep expectations that the human soul projects onto the sacred. By naming Him, the faithful not only acknowledges His greatness but also seeks to mirror within themselves the virtues these names evoke. There is, therefore, a movement of spiritual approach with each invocation: it is not about exalting an unattainable being, but about inviting His presence into the human experience.

By calling Mazda "He Who Hears Thoughts" or "Lord of Cosmic Order," man reminds himself that his thoughts matter, that his actions shape realities, and that there is a supreme principle attentive to the innermost part of his journey. These names, far from freezing the mystery, make it dynamic. They are not magic formulas, but portals to self-knowledge and alliance with truth. In each of them, there is an invitation to practice: act like one seeking wisdom, think like one desiring justice, live like one possessing clarity.

Zoroastrianism, by using these titles in rituals and prayers, teaches that language has power—and that the way we address the divine shapes the way we address life. There is no contradiction between the sacred and the everyday, because every simple gesture can contain the reverence of a name spoken with truth. It is in this simplicity that the greatness of Ahura Mazda manifests most fully. He does not demand formulas, but pure intention. And by allowing His diverse names to flourish on the lips of those who seek Him, He offers distinct paths to the same destination: the union between the awakened mind and universal order. Each title is a mirror reflecting Mazda's light from different angles, and whoever contemplates them with sincerity discovers that, in naming the divine, they are also naming what is highest within themselves.

Chapter 6
Angra Mainyu

Creation breathes in harmony, but this breath is restless, for it is never free from threat. At the heart of Zoroastrian reality, there is an abyss that never ceases trying to swallow the light. This abyss has a name: Angra Mainyu. He is not a metaphor, nor a philosophical symbol of antagonism. He is a real, conscious, and active presence. His essence is destruction, and his purpose is the negation of everything Ahura Mazda created with order and wisdom.

Angra Mainyu, the Evil Spirit, is the direct antithesis of Spenta Mainyu, the Benevolent Spirit emanating from Ahura Mazda. If the latter generates, protects, and orders, the former corrupts, destroys, and inverts. His origin is not easy to pinpoint, as he does not stem from Mazda. He is, in a way, a choice that became incarnate. A 'yes' transformed into 'no.' An intelligence that opted for absolute deviation. He is not a created entity, but a manifestation of that which rejects creation. His existence is not complementary to goodness—it is its negation. He does not balance the universe: he tries to disintegrate it.

The fundamental characteristic of Angra Mainyu is falsehood. Where there is truth, he insinuates doubt. Where there is trust, he sows betrayal. Where there is love, he feeds the ego. He acts in silence, for his strength lies in the subtlety with which he distorts reality. Falsehood, in his view, is not just factual untruth—it is departure from essence. When a man lies, he does not just deceive another. He harms the order of the world. He becomes an ally of the spirit that wants to dissolve all that is clear, cohesive, and pure.

Angra Mainyu's action in the world is not direct, but through influence. He has no power to create anything. Therefore, he needs to corrupt what exists. Disease, discord, envy, selfishness—all are expressions of his infiltration into reality. He does not destroy with brute force, but with slow degradation. He rots foundations, contaminates hearts, disfigures intentions. His victory occurs when human consciousness gives up choosing good, when it yields to moral fatigue and surrenders to spiritual apathy.

In Zoroastrianism, Angra Mainyu is a force that operates both on the spiritual plane and in material existence. He is behind the drought that kills crops, the lie that destroys families, the war that annihilates cities. Not because he is the creator of these events, but because he feeds on them. He manipulates circumstances to lead men to despair. His momentary victory happens each time someone renounces discernment and chooses the easy path—the one where good is postponed, justice is ignored, and truth is relativized.

But Angra Mainyu does not act alone. To multiply his influence, he generated evil counterparts to the Amesha Spentas. These spirits of destruction, called *daevas*, represent the distortions of divine virtues. Where Vohu Manah inspires good thoughts, a *daeva* whispers pride and vanity. Where Asha Vahishta sustains order, a corrupted spirit promotes chaos. They are like shadows following the light, trying to obscure it, imitate its form, and confuse those whose eyes are not awakened. These evil beings lack autonomy—they are instruments of Angra Mainyu's will, used as arms to extend his influence.

The struggle between Ahura Mazda and Angra Mainyu is not symmetrical. Mazda is not a warrior fighting an enemy of equal power. He is the origin, the foundation, the eternal light. Angra Mainyu is a crack, an aberration, a temporary rupture. However, his existence is dangerous because it acts upon human free will. Creation is good, but freedom allows one to deviate from it. And this deviation is the field of action for evil. Therefore, the fight against the Evil Spirit is waged not only in the celestial spheres but in the intimacy of each soul.

Zarathustra understood this truth with absolute clarity. The revelation of Ahura Mazda included not only the existence of evil but the call to confront it. The prophet made it clear that the human being is an active part of the cosmic battle. Every choice carries weight. Thinking well, speaking righteously, acting justly—all weaken Angra Mainyu. Every good action is a blow against chaos. Every honest word is a flame lit amidst the shadow. Zoroastrian spirituality is, above all, a call to moral vigilance.

This view of evil has profound implications. Evil is not essential to reality—it is a temporary distortion. It can be fought and will be, at the end of time, completely defeated. Zoroastrianism does not accept the eternity of evil. It will be vanquished through the combined efforts of the forces of good and human righteousness. When this occurs, the world will be renewed, purified, elevated to a state of perfection where Angra Mainyu can no longer penetrate. This moment of final victory is called Frashokereti. In it, the dead will resurrect, truth will be restored, and each soul will cross the Chinvat Bridge, where their deeds will be weighed. Angra Mainyu, then, will be expelled forever from creation. His illusion will be undone, his falsehood dissolved. And the world will finally be as Ahura Mazda dreamed it: pure, luminous, just.

But until then, the battle continues—not with swords or armies, but with the integrity of each heart. Angra Mainyu is the hidden adversary, the shadow accompanying every possibility. But he is not invincible. His weakness lies in the fact that he cannot create. He depends on human error, distraction, the abandonment of ethics. When men awaken, he retreats. When consciousness aligns with Asha, he is exposed. His strength is in confusion—therefore, clarity is his greatest enemy.

Behind the appearance of a fearsome and immutable enemy, Angra Mainyu reveals, deep down, an inherent fragility: his impossibility of generating anything of his own, his parasitic nature. He needs creation to exist, even if only to subvert it. It is in this dependence that the key to his defeat lies. Unlike Ahura Mazda, whose light springs from Himself, the Evil Spirit has no source of his own—he only reflects, in a distorted way, what has already emanated from goodness. Like a shadow that does not exist without light, he subsists only as long as there is something to be corrupted. But when good becomes firm, conscious, and determined, his influence withers, unable to withstand the presence of true order.

Inner clarity, therefore, becomes the most effective tool in the fight against this deceitful force. Recognizing evil not as an autonomous power, but as a deviation from good, grants human beings immense power: that of restoring the world from within themselves. Every ethical gesture, however small it may seem, is a realignment with Asha, a sign that creation still breathes through the will of good. And it is in the repetition of these gestures—daily, discreet, often invisible—that Angra Mainyu is weakened. He cannot resist the intimate commitment to truth, nor the silence of a conscience that refuses to negotiate with darkness. This is the responsibility and greatness of the human spirit: not just to resist, but to actively choose. For evil does not reign where there is firm decision, where there is light burning, where the soul keeps its eyes turned towards what is pure. With every choice for justice, compassion, truth, the shadow loses ground. And thus, even though the battle still persists, the end is already announced: not as a final spectacle of destruction, but as the slow and steady return of creation to its destiny of fullness.

Chapter 7
The Cosmic Conflict

The Zoroastrian universe is a living tapestry, woven by invisible hands operating on distinct planes. Existence, in this perspective, is not a neutral flow of events. It is a field of perpetual tension. And in this field, two principles confront each other with silent and devastating intensity: order and chaos, light and darkness, Ahura Mazda and Angra Mainyu. The world is not the backdrop for this dispute—it is part of it. And every living being, especially the human being, is a fundamental piece in the outcome of the great cosmic conflict.

From the very beginning of the revelation received by Zarathustra, it was clear that creation is not adrift. Ahura Mazda created the world with purpose: to establish order, justice, harmony. His Benevolent Spirit, Spenta Mainyu, infused reality with goodness, wisdom, and discernment. The cosmos was designed as an expression of truth, with precise laws reflecting its divine origin. Nothing was made in vain. Each element—fire, water, earth, thought, speech—carries within it the seal of creative intention.

But where there is order, there is the threat of dissolution. Angra Mainyu, the Destructive Spirit, rejected this order. He is not an external opponent, coming from outside the system—he is the internal rupture, the conscious refusal, the negation of good. His existence is a reaction. He saw Mazda's perfect world and hated it. Not out of envy, but out of inability to bear integrity. And his decision was clear: to corrupt, harm, erase everything that was a reflection of Asha—the Cosmic Truth.

From that moment, the conflict was established. Not as a battle of equivalent forces, but as a desperate resistance of darkness against the advance of light. Angra Mainyu lacks the power of creation. Therefore, his strategy is to subvert what already exists. If there is love, he inflates pride. If there is righteousness, he whispers doubt. If there is clarity, he spreads confusion. He does not act like a warrior, but like a poison: insidious, imperceptible at first, devastating in its advance.

The stage for this conflict is threefold. It occurs on the spiritual plane, where the Amesha Spentas confront the hosts of *daevas*—the evil spirits serving Angra Mainyu. It happens on the cosmic plane, where nature struggles to remain pure against corruption. And, above all, it occurs on the human plane. For it is within the soul that the war intensifies. Every thought is a spark that can feed light or shadow. Every decision is a small battle with repercussions that transcend individual life. The human being, in this context, is more than a spectator. He is both soldier and battlefield.

Human consciousness is where Ahura Mazda and Angra Mainyu confront each other most furiously. The mind that thinks with goodness becomes a temple of light. The word that builds becomes a sword of good. The action that respects life and promotes justice is like a wall against the advance of darkness. But the reverse is also true. When a human being lies, betrays, oppresses, they not only fail morally—they collaborate with the enemy of creation.

This conflict is not just a spiritual metaphor. It expresses itself in history, in cycles of decay and renewal, in the falls of empires and silent revolutions. Each era has its weight of light and shadow. Each culture, its particular struggle between Asha and Druj. And the fate of the world is not predetermined. It depends on the accumulation of these choices. The more souls turn towards good, the stronger the dominion of truth becomes. When many surrender to evil, reality approaches fragmentation.

Therefore, Zoroastrianism does not teach resignation. It teaches action. It is not enough to meditate on good—it must be practiced. It is not enough to denounce evil—it must be faced with courage and discernment. Zoroastrian ethics is an ethics of combat. Not violent, but firm. Not radical, but absolutely clear. Righteousness is non-negotiable. Truth does not bend. Light does not accept dwelling in twilight to please shadows.

There is a destiny laid out, yes. But it is conditional. Creation was made to triumph. Ahura Mazda planned a glorious end: the Frashokereti—the time of renewal, when evil will be destroyed and the universe restored to its original perfection. In that time, the Chinvat Bridge will serve as the threshold for every soul, and the balance of truth will be relentless. There will be no possible appeal. What each chose, they will live. And evil, fully exposed, will finally be vanquished. But this end is not inevitable. It depends on the collaboration of the just, the awakened, those who keep the flame burning even in the densest nights.

Zoroastrianism teaches that each generation carries the duty to keep creation alive. Not just with prayers, but with deeds. The farmer who cultivates with respect for the earth, the judge who decides impartially, the teacher who teaches with patience—all are warriors of Mazda. Their tools are virtues. Their shield is awakened consciousness.

Angra Mainyu, meanwhile, works to prevent this end from happening. His project is the perpetuation of falsehood. He desires man to believe that evil is necessary, that injustice is inevitable, that goodness is naive. He manipulates structures, corrupts languages, insinuates that everything is relative. But Zarathustra's revelation leaves no room for ambiguity: good is real. Evil is also real. And choosing between them is the deepest form of spirituality.

The cosmic conflict, therefore, is not about power. It is about fidelity. Whoever remains faithful to the light, even in the face of loss, pain, loneliness, has already won the battle that matters. And this victory is not invisible. It reverberates in the order of the world. Every act of kindness tilts the cosmic balance. Every ethical choice strengthens the foundations of creation.

There is, then, an everyday heroism at the heart of Zoroastrian doctrine, which transforms the common into the sacred. It is not about spectacular feats or grandiose gestures, but about integrity sustained in the silence of small decisions. The true warrior of light is one who keeps their word when it would be easier to retreat, who acts justly even when no one is watching, who chooses good without expecting reward. This is the field where the conflict is defined: not in distant heavens, but in the intimacy of human consciousness.

The battle of the cosmos is fought with the word, with the gesture, with the choice. And this is what gives the human being immeasurable value—he is the link between the visible and the invisible, the point where the divine decides to trust. This trust is also a responsibility. One cannot claim ignorance. The truth has been revealed, and with it, the call. Neutrality is impossible. Omission is a form of concession to evil. In a universe where light asks for active collaboration, silence in the face of injustice is complicity.

Therefore, the cosmic conflict demands not just faith, but lucidity. Moral awakening is an imperative. It is not enough to know—one must want. It is not enough to want—one must do. Each generation is summoned to renew this pact with creation, to reenact the drama of discernment between Asha and Druj, between what sustains and what disintegrates. And eternity watches—not with impersonal judgment, but with hope.

Hope, after all, is the invisible thread running through the entire cosmic narrative. Not passive hope, which expects good to win on its own, but active hope, made of conscious choice and righteous action. This hope knows that darkness is noisy, but not eternal. That falsehood shouts, but does not remain. That evil organizes, but does not prevail against the clarity of good. And that is why the cosmic conflict, despite its intensity, carries within it the certainty of a luminous outcome—not because it will be easy, but because it will be just.

Chapter 8
Divine Creation

Creation is neither a fortuitous act nor a divine whim cast into the void. In Zoroastrianism, it is a conscious, meticulous, ethical gesture. Ahura Mazda, in shaping the world, sought neither entertainment, nor dominion, nor adoration. He created out of love for order, out of the necessity to manifest, in concrete reality, the eternal principles of wisdom, truth, and justice. To create is to extend oneself, to multiply into living and harmonious forms. And each stage of creation reveals more about the mind of the Creator and the destiny of the universe.

Zoroastrian tradition describes the process of creation as seven sequential acts, each corresponding to an aspect of reality and one of Mazda's divine emanations, the Amesha Spentas. This number, seven, carries an internal harmony, representing totality and balance. Seven days, seven virtues, seven pillars supporting the cosmic edifice. And not by chance, each of these stages reveals the depth with which Ahura Mazda intertwines spirit and matter, meaning and form.

In the first act, Mazda created the Sky. Not just the firmament as a blue ceiling, but as the divine space where order is established. The sky is the shield protecting creation from the chaos lurking beyond the world's borders. It is vast, silent, and serene, like the Creator's mind. Associated with the Amesha Spenta Khshathra Vairya, the Ideal Dominion, the sky symbolizes the just kingdom hovering above the world, inspiring humans towards equity.

In the second act, came Water. Source of life, mirror of the sky, element of purification. Water represents movement without destruction, strength that washes without harming. Under the protection of Haurvatat, Wholeness, it carries the memory of origin and the promise of continuity. In its fluidity lies the teaching that life must adapt without losing its essence. Every pure soul recognizes Mazda's voice in the sound of a river flowing freely.

The third act of creation was the Earth. Firm foundation, ground where steps gain meaning. Creating the earth was setting the pillars of manifestation. It is beneath its surface that the seed sleeps, that time writes its presence, that cycles renew. The earth is the womb of creation, fertile, patient, silent. Spenta Armaiti, Loving Devotion, governs it. And in it is inscribed humility: everything that rises will one day return to it, not as an end, but as a restart.

In the fourth act, Ahura Mazda created Plants. And with them, inaugurated nourishment, sustenance that requires no blood. Plants are silent gifts, offering life without violence. They grow towards the light but are rooted in darkness, reminding that ascent begins at the root. Ameretat, Immortality, presides over this creation. For plants, even when reaped, spread seeds, and in them lives the promise that life refuses to cease.

Next came Animals, the Creator's fifth act. The animal presence in creation is more than biological function—it is a symbol of the sensitive connection between beings. Among them, cattle are especially revered, representing innocence that serves without destruction, the life cycle that nourishes without aggression. Vohu Manah, the Good Mind, guides this sphere, reminding man that care for animals is an expression of wisdom and compassion. To kill out of cruelty, to exploit out of greed, is to cooperate with Angra Mainyu. To protect and respect is to ally with Mazda.

The sixth act of creation was Man. Not as a superior being by right, but as a conscious guardian of creation. Man was endowed with reason, speech, and will to cooperate with the divine. He is a bridge between spirit and matter, between heaven and earth. In his mind dwells the capacity to choose, and in this choice resides the highest form of freedom and risk. The human being is called to reflect Ahura Mazda's light through just thoughts, true words, and pure actions. His existence is sacred because he participates in the world's destiny. He is both spectator and protagonist of the cosmic drama.

The seventh and final act was Fire. Not the fire that destroys, but that which illuminates and purifies. Zoroastrian fire is the visible presence of the invisible. It is not an object of worship, but the tangible sign of truth that burns without consuming. Asha Vahishta, the Supreme Truth, resides in this element. It is the guardian of consciousness, the filter of impurity, the lamp that does not go out in the heart of the just. That is why, on Zoroastrian altars, a flame is kept burning: to remember that the light of good is continuous, even when the night seems infinite.

These seven acts are not past events. They are structures of the present. The world is constantly being created because creation is sustenance, not just origin. Ahura Mazda did not withdraw after shaping the world. He remains, emanating His wisdom through the Amesha Spentas, renewing every moment, inspiring every being.

But this creation is under constant attack. Angra Mainyu, aware of his inability to generate, tries to infiltrate the stages of creation to deform them. He poisons rivers, contaminates the air, corrupts the earth with greed. He turns the mind into a battlefield, words into instruments of falsehood, actions into vehicles of selfishness. The battle for creation is permanent. And it falls to man, as part of this creation and a free agent, to decide on which side he will act.

Therefore, every element of the world is also a sacred field. Caring for the soil, the waters, the animals, is a form of worship. Preserving truth, respecting life, living with simplicity and dignity is keeping creation alive. Creation is not something that occurred in a mythical time—it is happening now. And it can be strengthened or wounded at every moment, according to human actions.

Zoroastrian spirituality does not propose escape from the world. It proposes absolute presence. To be in the world with consciousness, seeing every part of reality as bearing meaning and dignity. The universe is not an accident. It is a divine organism. And every creature, every gesture, every word is a stitch in this fabric.

This perspective lends existence a character of continuous reverence. To live is to participate in the maintenance of the cosmos. The everyday becomes sacred when permeated by the perception that everything is interconnected—the gesture of planting a tree, the choice of an honest word, the care for an animal, or the silent gratitude when drinking clean water. Nothing is too small when living within a creation pulsating with the divine breath. True spirituality, here, does not isolate itself in temples but infiltrates the world and transforms every moment into an altar.

And that is why man does not merely inhabit creation: he collaborates with it or harms it, sustains it or betrays it. Fidelity to creation requires attention and courage. It is impossible to remain neutral before a universe that depends on us to maintain its integrity. Angra Mainyu manifests in negligent habits, in greed disguised as progress, in disrespect masked as pragmatism. Recognizing this is also accepting the ethical call pulsing in every detail of existence. There is no separation between ecology and spirituality, between ethics and devotion. Care for the earth is also care for the soul. And when man acts aligned with the principles governing the seven acts of creation, he transforms the world into an increasingly clear mirror of Mazda's mind.

To live justly, in this context, is more than obeying commandments: it is tuning oneself to the very rhythm of the universe. Zoroastrianism invites us to participate in creation as conscious artisans, as guardians of the light emanating from every being. And this light demands not miracles, but integrity. Because divine creation is still ongoing, and the destiny of the world remains intertwined with the quality of the thoughts, words, and actions of each one. Whoever understands this no longer walks alone—they walk with the very essence of the sacred beneath their feet.

Chapter 9
The Seven Immortals

At the living center of Zoroastrian spirituality, where the sacred unfolds into function and meaning, reside the Amesha Spentas—the Seven Immortals. They are not isolated gods nor autonomous figures in the divine hierarchy. They are, rather, pure emanations of Ahura Mazda, aspects of His creative intelligence manifested as cosmic and ethical principles. When Mazda created the universe, He not only originated matter and spirit but also imprinted His own essence in seven living, eternal, perfect forms.

The term "Amesha Spenta" can be translated as "Beneficent Immortal" or "Holy Immortal." These beings do not die because they do not belong to corruptible matter. They exist on a plane where time does not corrode and evil does not penetrate. Yet, their influences pour into the world, like spiritual rivers feeding all created things. They are conscious forces, operative intelligences, living presences. Each is simultaneously a spiritual archetype, an element of nature, and an ethical value. They are not confined to abstraction: they act.

The first of these immortals is Vohu Manah, the Good Mind. It is through Him that wisdom enters the world. He inspires just thought, clean discernment, reasoning that seeks compassion. Vohu Manah is present when the mind refuses to be corrupted, when it chooses righteousness even if error promises shortcuts. It is He who leads Zarathustra into the presence of Ahura Mazda, as the Gathas relate. Cosmically, Vohu Manah is associated with animals, especially cattle, a symbol of innocence and peaceful utility. The just mind recognizes the dignity of life and treats it with respect.

Next comes Asha Vahishta, the Supreme Truth. This is not truth in the relative or conceptual sense, but the ultimate structure of reality. Asha is perfect order, the alignment between what is and what should be. Where there is justice, there is Asha. Where there is harmony, there is Asha. Its domain is fire, a symbol of purification and light. Truth consumes falsehood as fire consumes the veil of darkness. To invoke Asha is to seek to live in tune with the essence of reality, without distortions, without moral shortcuts, without justifications for error.

Khshathra Vairya comes third, representing the Ideal Dominion. He is not just the concept of just government, but the force that establishes legitimate authority. His element is metal—hard, resistant, incorruptible. He is present where power is exercised justly, where leadership serves the common good and not vanity. In Khshathra, royalty becomes sacred, provided it is used as an instrument of order. He protects those who govern wisely and condemns those who usurp power. He reminds that all authority should imitate the cosmic structure: strong, just, subservient to good.

The fourth immortal is Spenta Armaiti, Loving Devotion. She is the closest to the earth, and also the quietest. Her presence is felt in humility, patience, daily care. She does not impose but sustains. She governs the fertile soil, a symbol of faith that nourishes and shelters. Armaiti is the spirit of the wise woman, the protective mother, the worker who sows. Her devotion is not passivity—it is firm resistance, fidelity that does not waver. She represents the strength of surrender and the power of service as higher forms of spirituality.

Haurvatat, Wholeness, is the fifth. She governs the waters, elements of healing, purification, and integration. Haurvatat acts where there is health, emotional integrity, balance. Her energy is that of completeness, of totality that lacks no excess. She is invoked in rituals of blessing, in requests for harmony. Her presence dissolves internal conflicts, pacifies emotions, aligns the rhythms of the body with those of the soul. Her water not only cleanses—it consecrates. Where she touches, reconciliation between the being and its origin flourishes.

Beside her is Ameretat, Immortality, guardian of plants and the continuity of life. If Haurvatat protects the now, Ameretat ensures the hereafter. She is in the cycles of nature, the resilience of forests, the seed that resurfaces after winter. Her spirit acts where life renews itself, where the end is overcome by permanence. She also watches over the souls of the just until the resurrection. Her action is silent but vital: without her, there would be no tomorrow. Ameretat is Mazda's answer to the threat of Angra Mainyu. She affirms, with her existence, that good is eternal.

The seventh aspect is Spenta Mainyu itself, the Benevolent Spirit of Ahura Mazda. He is not exactly one of the six Amesha Spentas but encompasses them all as source and principle. Spenta Mainyu is the direct emanation of God Himself. It is the spirit with which Mazda created the world. It is the force that infuses creation with goodness, freedom in human beings, and wisdom in those who choose good. He is the creative impulse that animates existence with light.

These seven immortals operate in unity. They do not compete with each other. Each occupies a specific place in the structure of the cosmos and the human spirit. Together, they form the sacred framework that sustains the world. To understand them is to understand how Ahura Mazda acts: not as a distant king, but as a light spreading in distinct rays, each fulfilling an essential function.

The Amesha Spentas also have ritual and devotional roles. Each can be invoked in specific prayers, according to need: wisdom, healing, protection, moral guidance. In Zoroastrian temples, the fire burns in their honor, for each flame is a reflection of the light each immortal carries. They do not demand sacrifices—they demand consciousness. They do not desire fear—they inspire fidelity.

They are not just spiritual entities. They are guides. They are living maps. They are active forces touching the visible and invisible worlds. The farmer who respects the earth is with Armaiti. The judge who weighs justly acts under Khshathra. The physician who heals truthfully approaches Haurvatat. The poet seeking clarity aligns with Vohu Manah. All who choose good, in any form, are their allies.

This alliance, however, occurs not just through specific actions, but through the way the human being configures their entire life in resonance with these principles. The Amesha Spentas are not distant, awaiting formal recognition—they manifest in every lucid gesture, every compassionate movement, every decision made responsibly. Zoroastrian spirituality understands them not as figures to be worshiped, but as realities with which one can coexist. Devotion, in this sense, is not limited to prayer: it is a way of being in the world. To live according to the Spentas is to tune oneself to the intelligence of the universe, to become a channel where the divine not only touches but transforms reality.

In an age where the sacred often hides beneath the noise of the ego, the Seven Immortals remain silent yet potent foundations of a possible spiritual path. Each invites the human being to cultivate within themselves what sustains the world: clarity of mind, righteousness of action, generosity of soul, humility of posture, integral health, hope in continuity, and openness to the spirit. They are ancient virtues and, at the same time, urgently contemporary. And that is why the Amesha Spentas do not belong only to a remote time but breathe in the now, wherever someone chooses to live with lucidity and truth.

By recognizing these principles as living presences, the human being repositions themselves before the cosmos. They no longer see themselves as a mere passenger in a strange world, but as a conscious participant in a larger project. The Seven Immortals do not impose themselves with miracles or dogmas—they insinuate themselves as an inner call, a reminder that it is possible to live with meaning, justice, and beauty. Following them is not surrendering to an external morality, but rediscovering, at each step, the spark of a Creator who entrusted man with the privilege—and the duty—of being a guardian of the light.

Chapter 10
Vohu Manah

Among the seven spiritual pillars supporting creation, Vohu Manah—the Good Mind—stands as the first reflection of Ahura Mazda's consciousness, the closest to the human soul, and therefore, the most decisive in the moral journey of each individual. Vohu Manah is not just an ethical quality, but a living, active presence that guides thought towards light, diverts it from falsehood and corruption, and whispers the directions of justice into the silence of the mind. In a universe where free will is the most sacred of human tools, Vohu Manah's action is the most essential.

His name, composed of the words "vohu" (good) and "manah" (mind or thought), reveals more than a philosophical ideal. Vohu Manah is the very structure of the correct mind, the mind that thinks with clarity, compassion, and wisdom. To think with goodness, in Zoroastrianism, is not an emotional choice—it is an act of spiritual courage. It is aligning oneself with the principle of truth before it manifests in words or actions. Vohu Manah inhabits this liminal space between thought and choice, being the first line of defense against the subtle advance of Angra Mainyu.

It was he, according to the Gathas, who led Zarathustra into the presence of Ahura Mazda. He was not an angel in the traditional sense, nor an external messenger spirit. Vohu Manah appeared as an inner illumination, a clarity that broke the veil of doubt, like a lantern lit in the dark cave of the human mind. Zarathustra saw the light of truth not in the heavens, but in his own understanding—and that understanding was Vohu Manah. Since then, all who seek righteousness must first traverse this same inner path.

Vohu Manah's action is deeply rooted in moral consciousness. He does not shout, impose, or seduce. He whispers. He suggests firmly. He leads without forcing. Therefore, his presence depends on active listening, a clean mind, the willingness to abandon pride and illusions. The mind seized by vanity does not hear Vohu Manah. The heart that fears truth does not recognize his voice. He speaks only where there is room for the real, where the search is not for convenience, but for justice.

Cosmically, Vohu Manah is associated with animals—especially cattle, which in the ancient world represented the basis of sustenance, docility, persistence, and mutual benefit. Caring for animals, respecting them, protecting their integrity was, and still is, a way of honoring Vohu Manah. Not through animal idolatry, but because living beings coexisting with man are reflections of his capacity to live with compassion and discernment. Abuse, gratuitous cruelty, exploitation are crimes not only against nature but against the just mind itself. In Zoroastrian traditions, cattle assume a symbolic role because their presence demands balance from man:

they need earth, water, human attention—but also give back food, strength, and companionship. The man who treats his animals well, who recognizes in them a portion of Mazda's creation, demonstrates that his mind has not been corrupted by selfishness.

This connection between ethics and daily life is the seal of Vohu Manah. He does not dwell in the halls of theory—he manifests in the living practice of righteousness. On the spiritual plane, Vohu Manah acts as the soul's first protector. At birth, the human being carries the potential to think with goodness. This potential is a seed planted by him. Throughout life, this seed can be choked by pride, hatred, and ignorance, or it can be nurtured with reflection, listening, and honesty. Living with Vohu Manah is a constant exercise: think before speaking, question before following, discern before acting. The mind is not a mirror—it is a battlefield. And the good mind is one that refuses to be a field for lies.

Prayers dedicated to Vohu Manah ask not just for intelligence, but ethical clarity. Not just for knowledge, but wisdom. For the mind can be sharp yet perverse. Vohu Manah does not tolerate cleverness serving vanity, nor logic justifying error. He is the purity of reason refusing to be the ego's servant. His presence is perceived in silent decisions, in thoughts no one sees, in intentions defining the paths of human destiny.

He does not walk alone. His action connects directly with that of Asha Vahishta, for correct thought leads to truth, and truth sustains the world's order. It also intertwines with Spenta Armaiti, for a mind that thinks well must bow humbly before what is just. Vohu Manah is the spark initiating the process, the first step on the path of inner enlightenment. Without him, no virtue can stand, no purity remain.

It is also through Vohu Manah that judgment begins. After death, when the soul crosses the Chinvat Bridge, it is thoughts that will be weighed first. The good mind, if cultivated, will be like wings supporting the crossing. The corrupted mind, on the other hand, will be the weight dragging the soul into the abyss. Therefore, living with Vohu Manah is not just a moral issue—it is preparation for eternity.

Those who follow this path do not become unattainable saints. They become conscious beings. The good mind is not the absence of error—it is the constant presence of repentance and correction. It is not innate purity—it is daily conquest. It is the effort to look at oneself without masks, to think before acting, to choose good even when evil seems easier. In a world seduced by speed, noise, and appearance, Vohu Manah is the call to slowness, listening, essence. He is not exclusive to the religious or learned. He manifests in the peasant planting honestly, the child choosing truth, the elder teaching patiently. Vohu Manah lives where there is dignity in thinking. His presence depends not on grand rituals, but on small conscious gestures. He is the reminder that the world changes first within the mind. And that the just mind is the first form of light that can overcome, every day, the invisible assault of Angra Mainyu.

This silent light that Vohu Manah kindles in the human mind does not impose itself with fanfare, but shines deeply where there is willingness for self-knowledge. In a time when ideas become weapons and discourse often strays from reality, this Immortal's presence acts as an antidote against the arrogance of the soulless intellect. He invites a return to the essential: to think as one who serves, not as one who dominates; to reason as one who wishes to heal, not to win. Because the good mind is not just lucid—it is compassionate. And this meeting between clarity and empathy transforms thought into an instrument of redemption.

Perhaps this is why Vohu Manah is the most intimate of the Amesha Spentas. He does not dwell on distant altars nor demands extraordinary vocations. He stands at the door of every reflection, waiting to be chosen. His dwelling is intention; his temple, awakened consciousness. To live with him is to exercise the most difficult of tasks: sustaining good even when no one is looking, refusing shortcuts even when fatigue invites negligence. The good mind is not a gift received once, but a practice renewed each dawn.

Following Vohu Manah is, therefore, following a path of moral lucidity and active serenity. It is taking on the task of being a source of clarity in a world often overtaken by shadows. It is making the mind a mirror where Ahura Mazda's reflection can appear, even if fleetingly, with sharpness. And, in this constant choice for good thinking, man becomes co-author of creation—not just living in the world, but helping sustain it, thought by thought, gesture by gesture, like one who, by caring for their own mind, cares for the destiny of the universe.

Chapter 11
Asha Vahishta

If Vohu Manah is the seed of just thought, Asha Vahishta is the field where this thought takes root and blossoms as an integral life. Asha, a word whose depth finds no exact mirror in another language, means more than truth. It is truth as ordered reality. It is also righteousness, justice, purity, harmony, the rhythm of the cosmos when in its correct cadence. And Asha Vahishta—"the Best Truth"—is the supreme emanation of this principle in living form, one of the seven manifestations of Ahura Mazda, sustainer of the world and of awakened consciousness.

Asha is not concept, doctrine, or idea. It is the very backbone of reality. It is through it that the world remains stable, coherent, breathing in balance. When the sun rises each morning, when fire consumes impurities and reveals clarity, when the just word rescues a soul from confusion—Asha Vahishta is present. Its action is the purest of all because it seeks nothing for itself. It does not judge with feelings, but with precision. Its criterion is absolute: either something is aligned with order, or it is not.

Asha's presence is perceived in the rhythm of nature. In the flow of seasons, the return of rain to dry earth, the blooming of a flower in a rock crevice. Everything that repeats with exactness, everything born in conformity with its essential purpose, is under Asha's governance. The universe is not chaos. Chaos is the shadow cast by Angra Mainyu's action upon creation. Reality, in its original and full state, is Asha. And the role of the human being is to align their life with this flow, like a river running to its destiny without resisting the natural course.

In Zoroastrianism, living according to Asha is more than being good—it is being real. Falsehood is considered the greatest corruption because it not only deceives: it harms the structure of the cosmos. Lies, disorder, imbalance are not just moral errors, but affronts to the very fabric of creation. This is why Asha Vahishta is also linked to fire. Fire not only illuminates, but reveals. It burns illusions, transforms the impure, warms the cold of indifference. In the Zoroastrian temple, where the sacred flame never goes out, it is Asha's presence burning in silence.

The association of Asha with fire is one of the most powerful images in Zoroastrianism. Fire is not worshiped but revered as a living symbol of moral light. It never accepts the false. It does not simulate heat: either it warms, or it is not fire. It consumes what lacks essence. Similarly, Asha does not negotiate with falsehood. Its justice is precise, but not punitive—it is revealing. Whoever lives in truth does not fear Asha. Whoever hides in shadows, on the other hand, cannot bear its presence.

Asha Vahishta's action is not limited to the physical universe. It also operates in the human world, in social structures, in ethical judgments, in the consciousness that accuses and redeems. The judge who weighs impartially, the ruler who distributes equitably, the teacher who teaches without manipulation, all act under Asha's inspiration. She is the just measure in all things. The middle way, not out of timidity, but out of exactness. Living with Asha is being just without harshness, true without cruelty, pure without vanity.

She also has a decisive role after death. When the soul presents itself before the Chinvat Bridge, it is Asha that defines the width of the crossing. Good intentions are not enough—one must have lived in conformity with order. The soul's balance is not tipped by desires, but by actions. Asha is the criterion, the ruler, the mirror. There is no lying to her. What one was will be revealed. What one did will be measured. She is the memory of creation and the witness of each being's path.

But one should not fear Asha. She is beauty and perfection. The just man loves her as one loves music that moves, the perfect line of a work of art, the silence preceding truth. She is not a cosmic police officer—she is the harmony from which we all came and to which we all must return. Her followers are not those who bow in fear, but those who stand tall with dignity. Living with Asha is walking with the universe, without resistance, deceit, or disguise. In the human body, she is in the pulse of breath, the clarity of gaze, the firmness of word. She is in the gesture that needs no justification, the choice that does not doubt, the answer that does not waver. In the world, she is in the flower blooming unseen, the rain falling unasked, the time passing ceaselessly. Everything that does not lie, mask, or betray its origin—carries the mark of Asha Vahishta.

She also guides the rituals. In the Yasna, the main liturgical office of Zoroastrianism, the invocation of Asha is constant. Its spoken formulas, repeated in precise cadence, are like a reconstitution of cosmic order through the word. When priests recite the hymns, they are not just praising; they are realigning the world, purifying spaces, healing language. Language is, indeed, one of her most sensitive domains. Every uttered word must be true—not just in fact, but in intention. To lie is to break the link with the sacred.

Asha Vahishta does not demand perfection, but direction. She does not condemn the imperfect, but the one who refuses to walk. The just is not one who never falls, but one who always rises towards the right side. Error is not the end—it is the field of learning. But voluntary deceit, planned deviation, pretense—these are crimes against truth. Against Asha, nothing can hide.

Therefore, her presence in the faithful's life is a beacon. She shows what needs adjustment and offers light to do so. She is not punishment, but the path preventing punishment. Living with Asha Vahishta is the greatest shield against Angra Mainyu, who only thrives where truth is denied. Asha does not shout, but with her, everything resonates with meaning. It is in her that existence becomes melody, and chaos dissolves like a dream upon awakening.

There is something deeply comforting in knowing that the very structure of the universe pulses with the principle of Asha. Amidst the imperfections of the visible world, human deviations, and the shadows Angra Mainyu casts upon creation, Asha remains unchanged, like a golden thread running through time, available to anyone wishing to align with her. She does not demand grand rituals or painful sacrifices—she demands presence, clarity, and commitment to what is real. It is possible to live with Asha in the humblest of jobs, in the simplest of choices, as long as they are made with wholeness. She is the breath that straightens the soul when the world seems bent.

That is why Asha Vahishta cannot be conquered by arguments or bargains. She reveals herself to those willing to live truthfully in every act, even when no one is watching, even when truth seems costly. Because living in Asha is not being exempt from the world's pains—it is giving them meaning. It is understanding that every choice reverberates, that every lie breaks an invisible link between being and cosmos, and that every fidelity to truth, however small it seems, is a firm step towards completeness. Zoroastrian spirituality, by placing Asha as its axis, teaches that life's beauty lies not in the absence of conflict, but in the coherence with which one walks. And when the fire burns on the altar or in the heart, when the just word is spoken even at risk, when the difficult choice is made out of fidelity to what is right, Asha Vahishta manifests—not as spectacle, but as silent certainty. She is proof that a possible order exists, that good is not illusion, that truth is indeed habitable. And whoever chooses to walk with her may not avoid all falls, but will always find firm ground to rise again. Because Asha is, ultimately, the ground of reality itself: stable, clear, and ready to support those who decide, with courage, to live up to her.

Chapter 12
Khshathra Vairya

Amidst the luminous complexity of the Zoroastrian spiritual pantheon, Khshathra Vairya imposes himself not through brute force, but through the dignity of just power. His name, translated as "Ideal Dominion" or "Desirable Government," points to a dimension of divinity that encompasses the correct use of authority, the exercise of sovereignty in perfect harmony with truth, goodness, and wisdom. He represents power when it bows to good, not the tyranny imposed upon the weak.

Khshathra Vairya is not the lord of armies, nor the patron of territorial conquest. His dominion is that of the structure that protects, organizes, and sustains. He is the spiritual energy inhabiting the act of governing justly, the ethics that should guide leadership, the balance preventing power from becoming oppression. In an ideal Zoroastrian society, every form of authority—from home to empire—should reflect Khshathra. He is, therefore, a force that both inspires kings and regulates consciences.

On a cosmic level, Khshathra is associated with metal. And this symbol is not arbitrary. Metal, in its essence, is firm, lustrous, resistant to corruption. It does not yield easily to time. It has weight, presence, utility. In the spiritual universe, metal represents integrity that does not bend under pressure. The ideal ruler is like metal: malleable only to the right degree, but incorruptible in essence. He is a shield against chaos and a sword against injustice. Metal does not ignite like fire, dissolve like water, or move like air—it supports, anchors, builds.

Khshathra Vairya manifests where there is order, where law is an instrument of equity, where power is used to protect the innocent and maintain the coherence of social life with the eternal principles of creation. His spirit acts in the legislator writing clearly, the judge applying impartially, the leader serving the people without arrogance. Any authority seeking only itself, feeding on exploitation, or maintained by falsehood, is outside Khshathra's domain—and therefore, outside the alliance with Ahura Mazda.

Khshathra's spiritual function is not limited to political structures. He also dwells in the soul that knows how to govern itself. Self-mastery, discipline, strength of character, resilience against evil—all are expressions of his power. A man who masters his passions, who does not bow to despair, who resists the temptation of corruption even when unobserved, already acts under this immortal's influence. True government begins within: only he governs the world who first knew how to govern his own being.

Prayer to Khshathra Vairya is a request for strength with righteousness, influence with purpose, the capacity to protect without destroying. It is a call to responsibility. He teaches that having power is not synonymous with dominion over others, but with duty before the cosmic order. The ruler, the father, the teacher, the judge, the priest—all, to some degree, carry the burden and gift of power. And all must ask: does this power reflect Ahura Mazda's light or serve the ego masked as authority?

In the social body, Khshathra Vairya acts as a defender of distributive justice. He rejects unmerited privileges, structural inequalities, and systems sustaining the suffering of many for the benefit of few. His vision is of the community as an ordered body, where each member has value, and none is exploited. His presence is felt where the law does not favor the strong but protects the fragile; where progress is measured not by wealth, but by equity. He teaches that there is no lasting peace without justice, and that true power need not impose itself—it is recognized by its nobility.

Khshathra also plays an essential role in the judgment of souls. Alongside Asha Vahishta and Rashnu, the spirit who weighs deeds, he participates in the process measuring the merit of each existence. His balance measures not empty intentions, but fidelity to good in the exercise of will. A soul that had power but used it for self-benefit sinks during the crossing of the Chinvat Bridge. But one that, even with little influence, acted justly and promoted order, is lifted by this immortal's presence.

Among Zoroastrian faithful, Khshathra Vairya is invoked in times of moral crisis, in moments of decision where strength must be used wisely. He inspires ethical leaders, those who shape laws, and those who care for society's cohesion. But he is also an intimate counselor to the one who, alone in the silence of their decisions, needs reminding that governing oneself is the first duty.

His spiritual image, though invisible, is felt as a presence of silent firmness. He is not impetuous, demands no worship. But his absence is palpable in chaos, tyranny, corruption. Where there is no Khshathra, order becomes oppression, justice turns into an instrument of revenge, and power, a blind idol. Recognizing him is restoring authority to its sacred meaning. There is no true leadership without sacrifice, service, righteousness.

In the cycle of creation, Khshathra Vairya sustains stability. He maintains the pillars unseen, the foundations unmoved. The world may change, forms of government may vary, but the principle of just power is eternal. He existed before thrones, written laws, history. He is a living idea in Ahura Mazda's heart, shared with those who dare to lead without forgetting to serve.

Khshathra Vairya, therefore, not only outlines the ideal of external government but impresses upon the fabric of human existence the urgency of an non-negotiable ethical commitment. His influence reaches the everyday gesture and the grand decision, hovering over councils of state and whispering in the intimacy of solitary choices. He reminds that true sovereignty blossoms not in palaces nor rests on golden scepters, but germinates in the fertile ground of awakened consciousness. It is when power bows before duty that

Khshathra reveals himself most clearly—not as a distant entity, but as the very form of justice exercised.

This immortal's presence invites a reconfiguration of the idea of authority. In times where brute force and manipulation are often mistaken for leadership, Khshathra Vairya emerges as an essential counterpoint: a silent appeal for coherence, for structures serving the common good, for voices governing with listening, not imposition. Just as metal is forged by fire but not lost in it, the true leader is tempered by trials but remains whole. Through him, power gains contours of service, and greatness is measured by the capacity to sustain justice when it seems most fragile. The image of Khshathra Vairya, therefore, is not that of an unreachable throne, but of a force silently supporting the foundations of the just world. He does not cry for glory but demands courage; he does not impose himself by presence but is recognized by the order his absence compromises. And thus, all leadership aspiring to be worthy, every heart yearning for righteousness, finds in him not just an ideal, but a path—a constant call to remember that power is sacred only when born from good and living for good.

Chapter 13
Spenta Armaiti

In a world built upon the light of wisdom and order, there is a presence that leans down with gentleness to touch the ground of existence: Spenta Armaiti. She is Loving Devotion, the quietest among the Immortals, and perhaps for that reason, the most intimate. While the other Amesha Spentas rise as cosmic pillars—mind, truth, dominion, wholeness, immortality—Armaiti bows. She does not impose; she welcomes. She does not manifest in flashes, but in roots. Her domain is the earth, and her spirit is the humility that sustains the world without ever demanding recognition.

The name "Spenta Armaiti" carries a depth that escapes literal translation. "Spenta" denotes sacred growth, beneficial expansion, and "Armaiti" is the inner disposition of reverence, devotion, and peace. Together, these words form a principle that is not just religious, but existential. Spenta Armaiti represents the spiritual attitude of one who serves truth not out of fear or interest, but out of love for order, communion with good, silent fidelity to what is just. She is the fertile soil of the awakened soul.

In divine creation, Armaiti was given the role of guarding the Earth. The earth as a physical element—matter that supports steps, nourishes, receives the dead—but also the symbolic earth, place of spiritual cultivation, discreet service, silent fidelity. Her strength lies not in movement, but in firmness. She is the immobility that nurtures. What grows in her does not shout, accelerate, or explode—it blossoms. And so too is her action in the world: vital, deep, invisible.

The devotion Armaiti inspires is neither blind nor dogmatic. It is not passive submission to the divine. It is a conscious, loving, and humble alliance with the will of Ahura Mazda. She teaches that serving good is not humiliation, but elevation. That bowing before truth is rising before falsehood. She is the spirit that accepts life's lessons with patience, that does not despair in the face of time, that knows every seed blossoms if rooted in the right earth.

In human life, Spenta Armaiti manifests in all forms of care. In the farmer who plows the land with respect, the mother watching over her child in silence, the elder advising without vanity, the worker fulfilling their task with dignity, even without applause. She is present where there is service without vainglory, effort without pride, love without demand. The modern world, with its haste and vanity, has often forgotten Armaiti—and therefore, so often, the ground of existence seems barren.

She is also the spiritual model for the Zoroastrian faithful. It is not just about believing, but about living in active reverence to the cosmic order. True faith, according to Armaiti's influence, is not repeating formulas, but embodying principles. Loving devotion is, above all, coherence. The man who speaks of truth but lies; who praises good but exploits; who preaches light but acts in shadows—does not walk with Armaiti. His faith is hollow. But the one who, even without elaborate words, cultivates goodness in daily life, already dwells in her domain.

She is linked to silence. A silence that is not absence, but fullness. The silence of one who listens before responding. Who welcomes before judging. Who becomes ground for another to walk upon. In Zoroastrian tradition, there is a sacred respect for the earth—not just as a natural resource, but as a manifestation of Armaiti. Therefore, burying the dead with care, not harming the soil violently, thanking the food that comes from the earth—all are acts of devotion. They are forms of dialogue with her.

Spenta Armaiti is also present in true humility. Not the false modesty seeking praise, but humility as a state of being. The recognition that good depends not only on personal effort but on connection with something greater. She is the antidote against spiritual arrogance, against the belief that virtue is one's own merit. The just, for Armaiti, is one who knows their righteousness is the fruit of an alliance with the divine—and therefore, gives thanks, serves, remains firm even in adversity.

She is also a spiritual mother. She does not generate bodies, but sustains lives. It is in her that growth is possible. Therefore, those who turn away from her become spiritually sterile: they speak much but produce little. They seem wise but do not touch. They seem strong but do not sustain. With Armaiti, every action gains roots. She teaches that the true spiritual path is lived from the inside out, with patience, surrender, truth.

In times of instability, prayer to Spenta Armaiti is a return to the center. A reunion with the essential. She does not promise spectacular miracles but offers strength to continue. Peace that does not depend on circumstances. Firmness born of silent faith. She is the ground that does not yield. The womb that generates hope. The rock supporting the invisible temple of the soul.

She also acts in the final passage. When the soul leaves the body, it is the earth that receives it. And the way the earth welcomes it depends on how one lived with her. Armaiti does not forget. She knows the steps of each one. Knows who harmed the soil for greed, who respected it with gratitude. And when the time comes, she is the guardian of rest—or the witness of lack of peace.

Spenta Armaiti does not impose. She waits. Like the earth, which receives everything without complaint, which transforms everything in silence. And that is why she is so essential. For without her, there is no root, no permanence, no continuity. Without her, knowledge becomes pride, truth becomes a sword, power turns into oppression. She is the balance preventing good from getting lost in its own strength.

The presence of Spenta Armaiti reveals that spiritual greatness is measured not by speeches or extraordinary deeds, but by the humble constancy with which good is lived. She is the spirit of silent perseverance, of faith demanding no proof, of generosity seeking no reward. Her action is like rain softening the earth slowly, like time ripening fruits without haste. Where she dwells, the sacred becomes everyday, and the everyday reveals itself as sacred. It is under her influence that simple work becomes an offering, patience becomes strength, and silence becomes divine language.

By inspiring deep reverence for life in all its forms, Spenta Armaiti invites an embodied spirituality—one not limited to the temple but extending to how one treads the ground, treats others, awaits the right harvest time. She teaches us that serving is a privilege, caring is a form of wisdom, and true transformation begins in the inner willingness to listen and welcome. Her devotion is not an escape from the world, but a total surrender to its healing. Therefore, whoever walks with Armaiti does not flee challenges, but transforms them into a garden, even if the soil is arid.

In the silence of Spenta Armaiti rests the promise of a world sustained by tenderness. She does not raise walls or wield swords, but lifts lives with the serene power of fidelity. In her domain, everything profound grows in silence—like roots, like wisdom, like true love. And it is in this fertile space, invisible to hurried eyes, that the awakened spirit blossoms: not the one shining to be seen, but the one illuminating because it loves.

Chapter 14
Haurvatat

In the divine cycle structuring Zoroastrianism, there is an emanation that not only completes but harmonizes all others: Haurvatat, Wholeness. She is not merely the end of a process, but the spiritual state where everything integrates—body, mind, spirit, creation. Where Vohu Manah guides thought, Asha establishes truth, Khshathra shapes justice, and Armaiti roots devotion, Haurvatat weaves it all into a whole, integral being, living in harmony with oneself, with others, and with the cosmos. She is the seal of good lived and the expression of what is holy in total form.

Her name, in Avestan, literally means "integrity" or "totality." But the meaning she carries surpasses the simple joining of parts: it is a state where there are no internal fissures, moral contradictions, or spiritual dissonances. Haurvatat is the health of the soul reflected in the health of the body and balance with nature. She represents healing, not as a specific act, but as a way of existing. Where she settles, life flows without resistance, like a river recognizing its own course.

Haurvatat's elemental sphere is water. Water as source, purification, sustenance of life. Water that bypasses obstacles, fills voids, molds itself without losing essence. It flows through rivers, bodies, cycles of existence. It cleanses not only the body but the energy field, diseased thoughts, poisoned memories. Haurvatat's water does not erase the past, but reconciles it. She is the purest symbol of regeneration and spiritual fluidity.

Invoking Haurvatat is asking for completeness, not as accumulation, but as integration. It is desiring that the disconnected parts of life finally find their place, that what was broken can be woven anew, that what is scattered returns to the center. It is the longing for a peace independent of external circumstances, emerging from a soul that has found itself, that no longer fractures between what it thinks, feels, and does.

This wholeness is inseparable from health. But, in Zoroastrianism, health is not just the absence of disease. It is being aligned with Asha, living in consonance with the rhythm of cosmic truth. The body is sacred because it is the soul's vehicle, the temple of consciousness. Mistreating the body—with excesses, neglect, vices—is distancing oneself from Haurvatat. Caring for it, with balance and reverence, is honoring her presence. Similarly, caring for water, protecting it, purifying it, is a form of worship.

In devotional practice, Haurvatat is invoked in times of illness, both of body and soul. Her energy acts as balm on old wounds, as light on dark areas of consciousness. She invites self-knowledge without judgment, reunion with what was left behind. Her blessings manifest not just as physical healing, but as reconciliation with life, with one's destiny, with the inevitable pains of existence.

She is especially present in purification rituals, where water plays a central role. Ablutions, ritual baths, blessings with running water—all these gestures are invitations to Haurvatat's presence. But she dwells not only in rites—she is also in simple cares: the glass of water offered to the thirsty, the bath given tenderly to the sick, the river preserved from pollution, the lake respected as a mirror of the sacred. Where there is respect for life's fluidity, there she manifests.

On the ethical plane, living under Haurvatat's light is seeking coherence. It is not dividing oneself among multiple masks. It is being whole in all situations. The man who thinks one thing, says another, and does a third—lives in fragmentation, and there is no peace where there is division. The woman who welcomes truth, even when difficult, and lives it honestly—already manifests Haurvatat in her being. Wholeness demands not perfection, but sincerity. Not victories, but full presence.

She also shares her action with Ameretat, Immortality. Together, they guard the mysteries of continuity, of time that does not devour but matures. Haurvatat sustains the now—health, integrity, totality. Ameretat ensures this totality is not lost, even in the face of death. Both operate in sync, like waters meeting in the same ocean. One nourishes the journey. The other guarantees the journey has a destination.

In Zoroastrian eschatology, Haurvatat plays a central role. When the Frashokereti occurs, and the world is purified of all evil, it will be she who reigns over the restored bodies. There will be health for all, peace for the just, harmony among creatures. Waters will be crystalline, souls transparent. There will be no diseases, because there will be no moral misalignments. Evil will have been overcome not just by justice, but by the reintegration of creation with its Creator.

But Haurvatat is not just a future promise. She is a possible presence, here and now, in the cracks of light piercing moments of consciousness. She lives in small encounters, unexpected reconciliations, mornings when breath seems to dance with life. She smiles when someone forgives. When someone returns home. When someone chooses to care for the body as an act of love, not vanity.

She is also a guide for the lost. The shattered soul, the torn heart, the confused mind—all have in her a path of return. There is no wound her water cannot touch. No solitude her light cannot bathe. She does not promise to erase the past, but to transform it. Through her, even pain finds place, even error can turn into wisdom. Nothing is excluded from wholeness—everything is transfigured in it.

Living with Haurvatat is learning to flow. Not retaining what has passed, not fearing what will come, inhabiting the now with total presence. It is being river, not dam. It is being body, mind, and spirit in harmony, even amidst pain. It is accepting that life need not be perfect to be sacred—it just needs to be whole.

This wholeness Haurvatat proposes is neither rigid nor unattainable. On the contrary, it is flexible like the water representing her: it adapts, molds, welcomes. She teaches that true integrity lies not in never breaking, but in knowing how to reassemble the pieces with tenderness and lucidity. Under her influence, even chaos finds rhythm. Every gesture aligned with good, every word that heals instead of hurts, every silence that listens before judging is one more drop in this ocean of fullness. The soul seeking Haurvatat does not isolate itself from the world but dives into it with surrender, reconciling the parts with the whole.

It is in daily coexistence that Haurvatat's action reveals itself most intensely: in how we care for our own health and the health of others, in respect for what sustains us, in responsibility for what we flow with and absorb. She is in relationships not built on masks, but on sincere bonds. She is in work done with purpose, rest honored without guilt, the choice to live wholly even in a fragmenting world. Under her light, existence ceases to be a sequence of survivals and becomes an experience of presence. She reminds that peace is not absence of conflicts, but deep communion with who we are, despite and because of what we live. And when this communion is reached, even for moments, Haurvatat smiles—not as a distant achievement, but as an intimate reminder of what was always available. For wholeness does not impose itself; it emerges. And when it emerges, it not only heals but transforms: eyes see more clearly, the heart pulses with more compassion, and life, finally, reveals itself as what it always was—a sacred gift to be lived with wholeness and love.

Chapter 15
Ameretat

In the invisible fabric linking the divine to the sensible world, there is a thread that does not break, even in the face of time, death, and pain. This thread has a name and consciousness: Ameretat—Immortality. She is the emanation of Ahura Mazda affirming, with serene firmness, that good does not unravel, that life is not vanquished by death, and that what was generated in truth remains beyond the ruins of time. If Haurvatat represents the fullness of the present, Ameretat is the security of the eternal.

Her name, from Avestan, literally means "non-death." But this definition, though accurate, is limited. Ameretat is not just the end of death as a biological event. She is the guarantee that true life—the one aligned with cosmic order, justice, and light—cannot be erased. Even when the body succumbs, even when time destroys forms, the essence living in Asha remains. Ameretat is this permanence. She is the link between the ephemeral and the eternal.

In creation, Ameretat is the guardian of plants. Not by chance. Plants represent, in the visible world, the force of life that insists, renews itself, returns even after being cut down. They are born from the earth's darkness, grow towards the light, seemingly die, but continue in seed. They are, therefore, living symbols of immortality. By caring for plants, the Zoroastrian man not only respects nature—he participates in the perpetuating life cycle, cultivates Ameretat's presence, honors the stubborn vitality of good.

She is the force behind what insists on existing with integrity. She is in the sprout breaking hard soil, the tree bending but not breaking, the field reborn after drought. She is also in the soul that, even facing pain, does not give up truth. Ameretat is what resists without aggression, what endures without making noise. Her eternity is not made of grandeur, but of fidelity. Everything that remains faithful to good, over time, is under her protection.

But she also watches over souls. After death, when the body returns to earth, it is Ameretat who guards the spark of true life. Those who lived in accordance with Asha, who chose Vohu Manah, who acted with Armaiti, are welcomed by her. She guides them to the time of waiting—the time between death and the world's renewal. In this period, souls do not sleep but are kept in a state of tranquil wakefulness, protected from corruption and oblivion. Ameretat is the living reminder that death is not end, but transition.

She is also the promise of the restored future. In the Frashokereti, when Angra Mainyu is defeated and creation purified, all the just will resurrect. Their bodies will be remade in perfection, their souls reintegrated into unblemished flesh, and they will live eternally in harmony with Ahura Mazda. Ameretat will then be not just promise, but manifest reality. Death will exist no more. There will be no decomposition, oblivion, or loss. Life will be whole and permanent.

This vision, however, should not be understood merely eschatologically. Ameretat acts in the present. She inspires all who live with lasting purpose. Those who plant trees knowing they won't harvest their fruit, who educate children with values that may only bear fruit after their death, who fight for justice knowing they won't see victory—they live with Ameretat. Immortality is not just not dying—it is living so that death cannot erase.

Ameretat also teaches the value of patience. For everything durable takes time to form. The plant does not grow in a day. Wisdom does not sprout without maturation. Good does not impose itself—it consolidates. She invites the human soul to think in terms of eternity, not urgency. To act responsibly for future generations. To live so that one's life is seed, not just fruit. She inspires the kind of faith that builds cathedrals—the one starting a work knowing it won't be seen completed, but beginning it anyway.

On the moral plane, living with Ameretat is cultivating values resisting time. Honesty unchanged by fashion. Fidelity unyielding to convenience. Justice independent of applause. Respect existing without needing reciprocation. The immortal soul is one that, even traversing existence's cycles, does not deviate from light. And this light does not extinguish, because it is rooted in what does not pass.

She is also solace in moments of loss. When a loved one departs, when an era ends, when a dream dies—Ameretat whispers that nothing is lost when lived truthfully. That sincere love does not die. That authentic friendship continues living, even when physical presence ceases. She guards the bonds born in Asha. She preserves what time cannot destroy.

In daily life, she manifests in small choices of permanence: caring for the garden, tending the home, respecting traditions nurturing the soul, silence amidst the haste devouring everything. Living with Ameretat is resisting the ephemeral. It is not yielding to anxiety. It is knowing eternity is not made of intense moments, but simple gestures repeated with love.

This eternity Ameretat embodies is not an escape from time, but its transfiguration. She teaches us that time is not life's enemy—it is its ally, when lived with purpose. What is done in alliance with good inscribes itself in another, deeper time, where actions do not disappear but become seeds for future worlds. Daily fidelity, silent love, care without witness—all are harvested by her, kept in her sacred memory, and returned one day to the renewed creation. Thus, living with Ameretat is writing with one's own life a gospel of permanence, where each ethical choice is a gesture of eternity.

By making life an offering to what does not pass, the human being becomes more than an agent of the present: they become a bridge between generations, a channel for wisdom resisting oblivion. Ameretat is alive in the mother telling old stories to keep roots alive, the elder planting with trembling hands, the youth choosing righteousness in a world of shortcuts. In all these, she manifests as a tranquil force building without haste and remaining even when the world's lights go out. Her presence is like the green insisting among stones, the fragrance lingering in absence—discreet, yet undeniable.

And it is through this serene and resilient nature that Ameretat never needs to assert herself: she simply is. Her action does not clamor for recognition, but for continuity. Whoever lives under her influence understands that dying is not being forgotten, just as living is not merely breathing. True life is aligning with what never corrupts, never extinguishes. And therefore, by cultivating this inner life that remains, the being becomes part of what does not die—and finds in Ameretat not just a promise, but a dwelling place.

Chapter 16
Spiritual Hierarchy

In Zoroastrianism, the universe is neither a cluster of independent existences nor chaos governed by unpredictable wills. It is an ordered organism, a living spiritual structure where each entity has a specific and sacred function. Ahura Mazda's creation not only produced beings and elements: it defined places, roles, responsibilities. Within this worldview emerges the spiritual hierarchy—a subtle, organized network sustaining cosmic harmony and serving as a bridge between the human and the divine.

At the top of this hierarchy is Ahura Mazda, source of all light, wisdom, and truth. He is not just the creator: He is the active principle of order, the silent heart pulsating in all that is just. Everything emanates from Him, everything returns to Him. But His action is not solitary. He manifests through His conscious emanations, the Amesha Spentas, the Seven Immortals we already know as living facets of His essence. Each of these Immortals represents a cosmic, ethical, and natural principle, acting as an ordering force in a specific aspect of reality.

The Amesha Spentas, however, do not act in isolation. They operate in perfect unity, like different organs of the same body, like distinct rays of the same light. The structure they form is not one of command and obedience in the human hierarchical sense, but of functional harmony. Vohu Manah, Asha Vahishta, Khshathra Vairya, Spenta Armaiti, Haurvatat, Ameretat, and Spenta Mainyu form the backbone of the spiritual world. Together, they keep creation alive, just, and balanced. The combined action of these seven is what prevents Angra Mainyu from dissolving the universe's order.

Below—or more precisely, branching off from these—are the Yazatas, spirits worthy of adoration. They are numerous, diverse, and specialized. They were not generated directly as emanations of the divine essence but created by Ahura Mazda to protect, preserve, and cultivate specific aspects of creation. Their nature is benign, and their service incessant. Each Yazata has a particular domain: some govern natural forces like rain, wind, or fire; others care for moral aspects like justice, listening, spiritual vigilance. The Yazatas form the broad support network of the visible and invisible cosmos.

They operate on multiple levels: guarding elements, guiding souls, watching thoughts, orienting human beings. They are not worshiped as gods but revered as servants of good. Zoroastrian liturgy invokes them frequently, recognizing in them the active presence of the sacred in all spheres of life. Their action is an extension of Ahura Mazda's will, reflecting the diversity of forms without breaking the unity of principle.

In terms of structure, the relationship between the Amesha Spentas and the Yazatas is cooperative. The former represent the pillars of universal order. The latter, the builders and caretakers of this order in its most intimate details. For example, Asha Vahishta represents Supreme Truth, but it is through Yazatas like Sraosha, guardian of listening and vigilance, and Rashnu, the spirit of justice weighing deeds, that this truth is applied in the world and the soul. Khshathra Vairya represents the ideal dominion, but it is with Mithra, the judge of covenants, that this authority manifests concretely.

This spiritual hierarchy is not rigid, but functional. It reflects the idea that good is a network, not a pyramid. Evil, by its nature, tries to imitate this structure with its distortions. The *daevas*—evil spirits created or influenced by Angra Mainyu—also try to organize, but their system is unstable, lacking the cohesion born of truth. They compete among themselves, feed chaos, and seek to corrupt the order established by the Yazatas. But their strength is limited and temporary. The hierarchy of good, rooted in Mazda, is eternal.

On the human plane, this spiritual structure offers a model. Just as the cosmos is sustained by a network of cooperation and specialization, so too should be the just society. Zoroastrianism proposes not an authoritarian theocracy, but an order inspired by the values of the Immortals and Yazatas. The political leader should act like Khshathra Vairya, with justice and strength serving good. The educator should mirror Vohu Manah, guiding the mind with wisdom. The judge should channel Asha Vahishta, weighing deeds with clarity. The mother, farmer, artisan, priest—all have a sacred role, and all are parts of the great body of creation.

This hierarchy also serves as a guide for spiritual growth. The Zoroastrian faithful is called to align with each aspect of this network. Prayer, rituals, sacred days, festivals—all are oriented by the presence of the Immortals and Yazatas. By invoking each, the practitioner seeks not just protection, but alignment. Desires to be, to the human extent, a living extension of Mazda's will. The spiritual ideal is to become a microcosm of cosmic order.

At the same time, this structure reveals the pedagogy of Zoroastrianism: one does not reach the supreme directly, but in stages. First, cultivate the good mind (Vohu Manah), then righteousness (Asha), just action (Khshathra), loving devotion (Armaiti), inner health (Haurvatat), trust in immortality (Ameretat). Finally, union with the Benevolent Spirit (Spenta Mainyu) is attained. Each step is assisted by Yazatas who guide, protect, correct, and strengthen. The hierarchy is not obstacle, but bridge.

And like every true spiritual structure, this network is permeated by freedom. The human being is not condemned to a fixed role. They choose, daily, with whom they wish to align. Can serve good or collaborate with falsehood. Can be a link of order or a rupture of reality. The Zoroastrian spiritual hierarchy does not oppress—it inspires. Shows there is a place for everything, that everything can contribute to the whole, that the smallest gesture, if performed purely, reverberates in universal harmony.

This conscious freedom, while dignifying the human being, also summons them to responsibility. Within the spiritual hierarchy, there is no neutrality: every action, thought, and intention echoes in the cosmic fabric. Zoroastrian ethics is founded precisely on this intertwining of free will and the greater order. Thus, the individual becomes co-creator of reality by choosing, with lucidity and commitment, to align with the forces preserving and cultivating harmony. It is not blind submission, but enlightened adherence to a living truth manifesting both in the macrocosm and the everyday gesture.

In this sense, the proposed spirituality is not limited to the inner plane, nor to rite disconnected from practice. On the contrary, it invites total integration between being and acting, spirit and matter. Cosmic order is not just a model to be admired, but a call to be embodied. Each Yazata represents a concrete aspect of life, a field of action where the sacred infiltrates and can be recognized. The world, then, ceases to be a passive backdrop and becomes a dynamic field of spiritual relations, where awakened consciousness sees meaning, direction, and purpose.

Thus, the spiritual hierarchy in Zoroastrianism is not a chain of power, but a symphony of sacred functions. It does not impose limits but offers paths. It articulates the invisible with the visible, the eternal with the transitory, and invites the human being to occupy their place with dignity and clarity. More than explaining the cosmos, this structure sacralizes it—and, in doing so, points the human heart towards its true center.

Chapter 17
The Yazatas

In the spiritual architecture of Zoroastrianism, between the pillars supported by the Amesha Spentas and the invisible flows of Ahura Mazda's will, dwells a vast and intricate chorus of entities: the Yazatas. Unlike the Immortals, who are direct emanations of the supreme divinity, the Yazatas were created with the clear and precise mission to care for every detail of creation, every element of nature, every nuance of human and cosmic experience. They are the protectors of order manifested in its multiplicity, and although less known than the great spirits of the tradition, their presence is felt in almost every aspect of Zoroastrian life.

The word "Yazata" literally means "one worthy of worship." But this worship is not confused with idolatry. The Yazatas are not independent deities, nor rival intermediaries of divine power. They are servants of good, collaborators of the sacred, operative parts of the universal order. The adoration they receive is not for superiority, but for recognition: each Yazata is a living bridge between the visible and invisible worlds, between human gesture and the structure of reality.

Their origin dates back to the very creation of the world, when Ahura Mazda, shaping the cosmos in seven acts, also delegated responsibilities. Each Yazata was born with a function. Their mission is not generic: it is detailed, specific, linked to natural phenomena and spiritual values. Some are responsible for rain, harvest, night, truth, judgment, spiritual listening, fertility, the war against demons. Every aspect of reality finds, among the Yazatas, a protective consciousness.

The exact number of Yazatas is unknown. Some traditions mention thirty, others exceed this number, suggesting their multiplicity mirrors the very complexity of life. They appear in the liturgical texts of the Avesta, in daily prayers, religious festivals, and seasonal rituals. Their presence is constant, even when unnamed. The very language of Zoroastrianism is imbued with them: every ritual gesture, every revered element of nature, every recited prayer touches a Yazata.

Among the most revered is Mithra, spirit of sunlight and justice, the guardian of covenants, the silent observer of human promises. There is also Anahita, goddess of purifying waters and fertility, whose influence penetrates not only rivers and lakes but also the female womb and the subtle flows of emotion. Tishtrya, in turn, commands the stars and rains, fighting against the demon of drought. And Sraosha, who hears prayers, watches over souls, and guides them in the crossing of the world of the dead.

These Yazatas are not distant figures. They make themselves present in the elements shaping daily life: the sun that warms, the water that purifies, the wind that cleanses, the star that guides, the dream that reveals, the word that saves. Unlike religions centered on abstract and distant deities, Zoroastrianism offers a pantheon of proximity: each Yazata can be invoked, each responds to a concrete and spiritual need.

They are also warriors. Creation, constantly threatened by Angra Mainyu and his *daevas*, is defended by the vigilant action of the Yazatas. Some act in the invisible field, directly confronting the forces of corruption. Others protect humans from temptations, warn against error, purify spiritually contaminated environments. The struggle between order and chaos, far from being just a symbolic narrative, is lived by these spirits with absolute seriousness. Every victory of light over shadow is, in part, the fruit of the silent and tireless work of the Yazatas.

The relationship between the Yazatas and humans is based on reciprocity. They protect, inspire, heal, guide—and in return, ask only to be remembered with reverence, that their forces be honored, that the elements under their guard be treated with respect. Polluting waters is an offense to Anahita. Breaking an oath stains Mithra's field. Disrespecting the night, sleep, rest, assaults the domain of a Yazata of sacred darkness. Honoring them is living in harmony with the world.

This multiplicity, far from confusing, reveals the beauty of Zoroastrian unity: Ahura Mazda is one, but His light refracts into a thousand forms. The Yazatas are these forms, these distinct beams illuminating different parts of reality. The faithful who understand this do not get lost in dispersed worship but are strengthened by plural connection. Just as the human body has diverse limbs, each fulfilling an essential function, so too the spiritual body of the universe is made of these specific consciousnesses, all indispensable.

Zoroastrian festivals reflect this reverence. Each month is dedicated to a Yazata. Each day carries the energy of one of these entities. The names of the days, far from being mere temporal conventions, are living invocations. Waking up on a day dedicated to Tishtrya, for example, the faithful knows that moment carries blessings for agriculture, rain, projects requiring fertility. Time, thus, becomes sacred not by abstraction, but by spiritual presence.

The Yazatas are also figures of transition. They help human beings pass from one state to another: from ignorance to wisdom, pain to healing, illusion to truth, life to death, and death to eternal life. They not only protect but transform. Contact with them is not static—it is pedagogical. Each invocation is also a learning experience. The faithful becomes more just by invoking Mithra, purer by honoring Anahita, more vigilant by remembering Sraosha.

It is seen, then, that the Yazatas are more than protective spirits. They are spiritual instructors, guardians of order, and living instruments of Ahura Mazda's will. They make the divine tangible, make spirituality everyday, show that the sacred is in everything: in the sun's heat, the water's flow, the word's sound, the soil's firmness, the wind's movement. The universe is a temple, and the Yazatas are the invisible ministers keeping it lit.

This perception of the Yazatas as ministers of the cosmic temple profoundly broadens Zoroastrian spirituality, rooting the sacred in direct, everyday experience. It is not a faith solely focused on the beyond or the invisible, but a concrete experience where each element of the world reveals itself as an opportunity for connection with the divine. By recognizing the Yazatas' action in the order of time, the cycle of seasons, human bonds, and inner processes, the faithful learns to walk with reverence, perceiving that everything around them is imbued with purpose and presence. Spirituality thus becomes constant listening—an openness to the teaching each aspect of creation offers, mediated by these attentive spirits.

This teaching is not neutral: it leads to good. The Yazatas not only reflect order; they sustain it against the onslaughts of chaos. In each of them, Ahura Mazda's light acts as a force of resistance and regeneration. Honoring the Yazatas is not just venerating them, but also choosing their paths: commitment to truth, preservation of nature, honesty in bonds, inner listening, courage against evil. Each Yazata is a beacon lit amidst Angra Mainyu's temptations, reminding the human being they are never alone—that cosmic order is populated by attentive, active allies, willing to guide and fight alongside good.

By making this network of presences visible, Zoroastrianism offers not just a theology, but a living ethic. The Yazatas inspire a spirituality manifested in concrete gestures and daily choices. They teach that the sacred does not distance itself from the world—on the contrary, it penetrates it completely. And by recognizing this, the faithful awakens to their own vocation: to be, themselves, a conscious link between heaven and earth, a living extension of the order the Yazatas guard and cultivate with tireless love.

Chapter 18
Mithra, the Judge

At the heart of the Zoroastrian pantheon, where light pours into spiritual figures representing the multiple facets of truth, stands Mithra—the Yazata of covenant, sun, justice, and silent observation. He is more than a spirit of visible light: he is the consciousness that never sleeps, the judge weighing not public gestures, but inner vows, silent pacts, commitments made without witnesses. In a universe where order depends on fidelity, Mithra is the guardian of trust.

His name carries the weight of millennia. Derived from the Indo-Iranian root *mitra*, meaning "contract," "agreement," or "bond," Mithra is the invisible presence in every act of pledged word. He is invoked not only in religious or social pacts but in any commitment where truth and responsibility are involved. His function, however, is not just preserving external honesty: he probes intentions. He assesses the moral integrity of the one promising. It is not the oath that guarantees his blessing—it is the veracity with which it is made.

In Zoroastrianism, truth is not just a value—it is an ontological principle. The universe was created based on Asha, the supreme truth, and is sustained by it.

Therefore, lying, betraying, deceiving, are not just ethical flaws—they are acts that harm the very structure of reality. Mithra, as guardian of this structure, closely watches everything that could compromise it. He is the judge without robes, the all-seeing solar eye, who needs not be called to act: he acts, simply because truth is his dwelling place.

Mithra is also associated with the sun, not just as a celestial body, but as a metaphor for revealing light. The sun sees everything. No corner of shadow escapes its touch. Similarly, no pact escapes Mithra's gaze. He is not deceived by formal oaths or rehearsed gestures. He sees intention. He sees the thought preceding the word. He sees the action contradicting the promise. In his light, there is no room for masks.

This role as spiritual judge reaches its peak at the crossing of the Chinvat Bridge—the threshold between the world of the living and the dead. There, according to Zoroastrian texts, the soul of every human being is judged. And Mithra is present at this crucial moment, as one of the three cosmic judges, alongside Rashnu, the spirit who weighs deeds, and Sraosha, the spirit of listening and consciousness. Mithra not only observes what was done—he recalls what was promised, what was left unfulfilled, what was broken.

Mithra's judgment is not punitive, but revealing. He does not condemn: he merely exposes. The Chinvat Bridge narrows or widens according to the soul's truth. For one who lived faithfully, the crossing is safe. For one who lied, betrayed, and dishonored commitments, the bridge narrows until it can no longer support the weight of the corrupted soul. And then, the fall is inevitable. Not as punishment, but as consequence.

In the visible world, Mithra's presence is intensely worshiped. Specific rituals are dedicated to him, especially in celebrations involving alliances: weddings, community agreements, initiations. He is invoked to protect legitimate bonds, ward off falsehood, bless just commitments. In some texts, it is said that heaven itself vibrates when an oath is made in his name—and trembles when it is violated.

Mithra is also a figure transcending Zoroastrianism. His influence spread to neighboring cultures and was absorbed by later religions, especially in the Greco-Roman world, where it gave rise to the Mithraic cult. Although this cult developed its own characteristics, its basis traces back to the same essence: the worship of truth, the sun, just judgment. Mithra's figure became a symbol of the warrior of light, the mediator between heaven and earth, the redeemer confronting darkness. But in original Zoroastrianism, he remains a Yazata—not an independent god, but a sacred servant of divine order.

His strength lies not in weapons, but in moral clarity. He teaches that every word matters. That every promise is sacred. That every human relationship, if built on lies, will be corroded from within. And that good cannot flourish where truth is relativized.

Living with Mithra is living transparently. It is aligning word and action. It is fulfilling what one promises, even in silence. It is respecting bonds, agreements, limits. It is understanding that spirituality is measured not by elaborate rituals, but by daily fidelity. It is perceiving that each morning, as sunlight appears, is a reminder of the light that judges—and saves.

On days dedicated to Mithra, the faithful are invited to moral reflection. They review their alliances, pledged words, commitments to others and themselves. They seek to repair what was broken. Seek reconciliation with truth. These days are not just ritual dates—they are opportunities for restart. For Mithra is also merciful. He judges rigorously but loyally protects those trying to live with integrity. He is the spirit sustaining trust. And without trust, no society stands. No community flourishes. No love endures. No faith sustains itself. Therefore, his role is so crucial: he is the invisible foundation of just coexistence. It is he who maintains the link between what was said and what will be done. Between the human and the divine. Between today and eternity.

Mithra, therefore, embodies the ethical bridge between the sacred and the everyday, where each gesture of integrity reinforces the very structure of the cosmos. His vigilance imposes not fear, but lucid responsibility. He demands not fearful adoration, but deep commitment to authenticity. Under his solar gaze, masks fall, and the value of each soul reveals itself in the coherence between what is promised and what is realized. It is in this intimate space—where intention and action meet—that Mithra builds his dwelling and strengthens trust as the foundation of just life.

This trust, however, is not static. It renews, tests itself, rebuilds itself in the intertwining of human life with existence's rhythms. Mithra is the spirit accompanying each silent decision, each choice made outside the applause, each truth upheld even under pressure. He inspires a mature spirituality, made not of visible miracles, but of small daily fidelities. Therefore, his role surpasses rites and installs itself as a demand for coherence: he invites the faithful to transform the pledged word into a path, and commitment into luminous presence in the world. Following Mithra is accepting that true judgment occurs not at life's end, but in every instant one chooses between the false and the authentic. It is living under a light that does not blind, but reveals. It is recognizing that the most sacred pact is the one renewed daily with truth. And in this pact, Mithra remains—silent, firm, guardian of the invisible alliance between the soul and eternal order.

Chapter 19
Anahita, the Lady of the Waters

Among the most revered and recognized Yazatas in Zoroastrianism, a figure rises with grace and strength, carrying in her hands the power of life, fertility, and purification: Anahita, the Lady of the Waters. She is one of the most imposing female entities in Iranian spirituality, as ancient as she is venerable, a presence crossing the boundaries between the visible and invisible, myth and rite. Her water is not just liquid—it is spiritual, essential. It is the flow of blessing, the river traversing worlds, the source of regeneration.

The name "Anahita" can be understood as "the Immaculate," "the Pure," "the Unstained." This title immediately reveals her sacred nature and connection to absolute purity. Her domain includes running waters—rivers, lakes, springs, rains—but also the vital moisture sustaining bodies, seeds, and ideas. Anahita is not just a water goddess as a physical force: she is the spirit of universal fertility, the matrix of renewal, the lover of flowing truth. She is both mother and warrior. Welcoming like rain irrigating thirsty land, and impetuous like rapids sweeping away falsehood. It is through her waters that the earth opens to fruit, the womb conceives, the soul purifies itself. Every drop that cleanses, heals, fertilizes, consecrates, carries within it the memory of Anahita. And every ritual seeking to restore the balance of soul or nature invokes her, even in silence.

The ancient temples dedicated to her—some still recognizable in archaeological remains—reveal her centrality in Persian religiosity. In them, water sources were preserved as living sanctuaries. Priestesses and priests cared for purification rituals, offerings of flowers, chants dedicated to the celestial lady. No blood or animal sacrifice was offered to Anahita. Her language was beauty, clear water, careful gesture. She was honored with cleanliness, ornamentation, praise in the form of poetry.

Her iconography, at times, crossed the line between strict Zoroastrianism and external influences. She was depicted as a long-haired woman, crowned, with golden robes and chalice in hand—an image echoing in later deities of other pantheons. But for Zoroastrians, this image is not an idol, but a symbol: representing the beauty of fertility, the abundance of water, the sovereignty of the woman who is source, guardian of life and integrity.

Anahita governs the mysteries of female creation. Her domain touches the woman's body in its fullness: menstruation, gestation, childbirth—all considered, under her light, sacred processes. She protects mothers and children, watches over births, accompanies women's cycles as a silent, eternal presence. No aspect of the feminine, however hidden or rejected by social norms, escapes her protection. Woman, in her totality, is a living extension of her spirit.

But her action is not restricted to the feminine. She is also the force restoring dignity to the stained, those who strayed from good, the lost. Through her waters, the repentant can find themselves again. The purification ritual, performed with running waters, is more than symbolic: it is the visible practice of returning to the spiritual axis. Washing oneself in Anahita's name is declaring readiness to start over. No impurity withstands her current.

In the cycle of seasons, Anahita manifests in times of water abundance. Her festivals were traditionally celebrated during summer, when water becomes most precious. Rituals involved community baths, blessings with perfumed water, offerings of floating flowers. Even today, among contemporary Zoroastrians, especially Parsis, her memory is preserved with prayers and symbolic gestures of gratitude for water as a divine gift.

She also acts as a mediator between the human and the celestial. The water she governs is the bridge between worlds. Falling from the sky, it becomes divine response to supplication; emerging from the earth, it reveals the sacred also sprouts from within. Anahita's water is circular: it rises, descends, infiltrates, evaporates, returns. It is a reminder that spirituality is dynamic, that true life cannot stagnate. Everything must flow, including the soul.

She is associated not only with the element water but with the very principle of integrity. Her purity is not isolation, but transparency. She teaches that living truthfully is being like clear water: visible, honest, available. Lies, dissimulation, duplicity—these are impurities clouding the spirit. Under her gaze, no pretense endures. The soul wishing to commune with her must become limpid.

Anahita also represents a model of female spiritual authority. In a world often marked by masculine power structures, she imposes herself as a full, independent, active figure. Her strength derives not from confrontation, but fertility, the capacity to generate, nurture, transform. She shows that female strength is cosmic, not secondary. And that wherever there is respect for life, care for water, reverence for the cycle, her presence will be felt.

Her image has traversed centuries. Although her cult underwent transformations over time and cultural influences, her essence remains. In water that runs and purifies. In the womb that generates and guards. In the tear cleansing pain. In the bath renewing body and soul. In the silent promise that everything can be restored, as long as there is truth.

In Anahita's presence, spirituality assumes a gentle and deep contour, where the sacred silently infiltrates simple and vital gestures. Her strength does not shout, but floods; does not impose, but penetrates. Invoking her, one asks not just for material blessings—one asks for lucidity to recognize beauty in vulnerability, accept cycles humbly, allow the soul to be touched, washed, opened. Water, under her governance, is master of detachment: teaching to follow, yield, transform pain into movement. And with this, Anahita not only guides—she heals. Her restorative power reveals itself not only in waters running outside, but in inner waters, crying for emotional fluidity and spiritual clarity. She is in the reconciliation of affections, the purification of resentments, the rebirth of hope. Her cult, more than external practice, is an inner dive—a call to remove sediments separating us from essence.

As Lady of the Waters, Anahita reminds that integrity is a constant flow: requiring vigilance, surrender, sincerity. Being integral is, like water, finding one's own path even amidst obstacles, without ever losing transparency. Thus, Anahita remains a living symbol of the sacredness dwelling in the ordinary. She invites reverence for what sustains life on all planes—body, earth, spirit. Her lesson is clear: where there is purity, there will be strength; where there is care, power will flourish; where there is truth, everything can be reborn. And just as her waters never cease running, so too her presence will continue flowing, between rituals and silences, guiding those seeking regeneration along the path of beauty, delicacy, and fidelity to what is essential.

Chapter 20
Tishtrya, the Starry One

In the celestial vault covering creation, where stars twinkle like eternal eyes of the sacred, there is an entity watching the earth with a firm gaze and a just heart: Tishtrya. He is the Yazata of stars and rains, guardian of agricultural fertility, and implacable enemy of drought. In essence, Tishtrya is the spirit of restorative abundance. He not only governs the heavens—he intervenes in earth's cycles, intertwining high and low with his luminous and active presence.

His name resonates with the brilliance of Sirius, the brightest star in the night sky, whose rising marked times of change and hope in the agrarian traditions of ancient Iran. Tishtrya is not just a celestial body—he is the spiritual consciousness inhabiting this star, an emissary of cosmic order responding to the cries of parched earth. In times of drought, it is to him the faithful's cry is directed; it is his strength that summons clouds, opens heavens, makes the cycle of life turn again.

He does not act alone. Zoroastrian tradition describes his ritual combat against *Apaosha*, the spirit of drought, who tries to prevent the arrival of rains and thereby compromise life's continuity. This battle, waged not only in the heights but in fields and consciousnesses, is one of the clearest representations of the cosmic conflict between order and chaos. Each time rain arrives after long days of clear sky and arid soil, it is Tishtrya's victory manifesting. And each time drought persists, it is Apaosha trying to impede the flow of blessing.

This combat is not merely symbolic. It is spiritual, ethical, existential. For just as the earth's body can dry up, so too the human heart can become sterile. Tishtrya's absence signifies not only lack of rain but also hardening of the soul, absence of compassion, loss of trust in renewal. He represents, therefore, active hope—not the one that waits, but the one that cries out, invokes, acts with faith in the return of good.

In rituals, Tishtrya is invoked in moments of climatic need, especially during drought periods. Ancient and contemporary Zoroastrian communities raised specific prayers, chants, and offerings to reactivate his presence in the skies. The prayers, intoned in unison, sought to reestablish the link between earth and heavens, reminding Tishtrya of the sacred alliance between the celestial spirit and the guardians of creation.

In the moral world, Tishtrya symbolizes fidelity to life. He is the spirit ensuring aridity is never permanent, as long as effort is made to maintain balance. He inspires the farmer's persistence, the shepherd's patience, peoples' resistance against climatic and spiritual adversities. Living under his light is believing that, even after long periods of scarcity, abundance can return. But this return requires vigilance, ritual, conscious action. It is not automatic—it is the fruit of continuous alliance with cosmic order.

Tishtrya's figure also carries an archetype of the warrior of light. His battle against Apaosha is fought every year, every day, in all parts of the world. It is not a single mythical event, but a perpetual cycle of struggle and victory. Every drop of rain falling where there was despair is proof he still rides the heavens, that his presence still responds to justice. He is, therefore, more than a natural force—he is a spiritual principle: the good fighting against life's impoverishment.

His connection with stars is not accidental. Stars, for Zoroastrianism, are dwellings of the just, points of light in the sky reflecting souls' integrity and spirits' vigilance. Tishtrya, as guide-star, is also a beacon for travelers, for those crossing inner or outer deserts. His light guides. His brilliance consoles. His presence in the night sky is like a continuous reminder that, even in darkness, there is order. Even in silence, there is music. Even in aridity, there is promise of rain.

The sacred texts mentioning him—especially Yasht 8, one of the Avesta's most beautiful hymns—describe his form as glorious, luminous, with spiritual weapons piercing darkness and purifying heavens. He appears in three forms: as a brilliant white horse in the waters, a radiant youth, and a resplendent bull. Each form reveals an aspect of his mission: speed, purity, fertility. He is not limited to one appearance—he adapts to what the earth needs, what the human spirit seeks.

For contemporary Zoroastrians, Tishtrya remains a symbol of renewal and overcoming. His prayers are recited in times of climatic and personal challenge. His name is invoked in agricultural blessings, weddings desiring fertility, initiations calling for clarity on the path. His energy, though ancient, has not become abstract. On the contrary, it pulses each time a seed breaks the earth, rain bathes the skin, a soul decides to move forward despite surrounding aridity.

Tishtrya remains, thus, a celestial reminder that all scarcity carries within it the seed of abundance. His cult, beyond the request for rain, is also a call to active faith—a spirituality refusing to succumb to discouragement and recognizing, in the act of invoking good, a way to resist collapse. He teaches that renewal is not a random gift from heavens, but the fruit of continuous alliance between the waiting human and the responding divine. The sky, under his light, becomes a field of listening; the earth, territory of trust; and the soul, shelter of hope in motion.

Tishtrya's presence intertwines the visible and invisible with fiery delicacy. Each time rain falls on cracked earth, each time the star appears in the firmament after a period of darkness, it is as if he says chaos will never have the last word. He brings not just water: he brings memory and promise. The memory of a time when good governed cycles, and the promise that this time can return, provided there is alignment with sacred order. His brilliance in the night sky is the cosmic signature of perseverance, a luminous voice echoing silently: "It is still possible to flourish."

Living under Tishtrya's influence is learning to recognize cycles, respect the times of earth and soul, and act even when the horizon seems sterile. He is the rider of clouds, bearer of visible rains and invisible blessings, the one teaching that, facing dryness, one should not just wait—one should cry out, cultivate, and believe. Because, just as the star reappears in the sky and rain falls again, so too the human heart, when faithful to good, rediscovers its own fertility.

Chapter 21
Sraosha, the Guardian of Consciousness

On the threshold between sound and silence, wakefulness and sleep, the visible and the invisible, moves Sraosha—the spirit of listening, spiritual obedience, and vigilance of the soul. Among the Yazatas, his function is unique and essential: he is the guardian of human consciousness, the one who whispers divine truths into the inner mind, who watches over the most secret thoughts, who accompanies the human being from birth to beyond death. In a world where order can be threatened not just by actions, but by moral distractions, Sraosha is the sacred alarm, the living reminder of righteousness.

His name, "Sraosha," can be understood as "listening," but it's not just about hearing sounds. It is listening with the soul, the spirit, with awakened discernment. He is the spirit allowing human beings to perceive the voice of good amidst the world's noise, distinguish the true from the illusory, recognize the sacred call even when presented as silence. Listening, in the Zoroastrian perspective, is an active act. It is not passivity: it is readiness. And Sraosha is this divine readiness personified.

He is described in sacred texts as a warrior of light, armed with just words, enveloped in clarity, always in motion. He does not rest. Does not sleep. Is never absent. Always vigilant. His presence is especially felt during nighttime hours, when the world retreats, but thoughts continue to work. Nighttime, in Zoroastrianism, is spiritually perilous: *daevas* lurk around those sleeping with unattentive minds. It is then that Sraosha watches, guards homes, protects dreams, shields consciousnesses.

But his action is not merely defensive. He also instructs. He reveals. It is said that Zarathustra's teachings reached the world partly thanks to Sraosha's action, facilitating deep listening, preparing the inner ground for contact with truth. He is, therefore, the spirit of continuous revelation, not the one coming from outside, but the one sprouting from within. He invites man to listen not to the world, but to what the world hides. Not the noise, but the music behind the noise.

In the soul's journey after death, Sraosha plays a decisive role. He accompanies the soul for the first three days and nights, protecting it from evil spirits trying to divert, confuse, imprison it. He is the secure presence in the unknown. It is with him that the soul moves to the Chinvat Bridge, where it will be judged. Along this path, his voice resonates as guide, solace, clarity. The soul that listened to its conscience in life recognizes his voice after death. And is guided with confidence.

Sraosha's spiritual iconography shows him as a being of uncommon beauty, white robes, attentive eyes, firm as the truth he represents. His weapon is the word.

His shield, listening. He does not destroy with violence, but with revelation. He does not win by force, but by presence. His mere proximity transforms space: where he enters, falsehood falters, hatred falls silent, the ego quiets. He is, therefore, as feared by the *daevas* as loved by the just.

His connection with the word is profound. In Zoroastrianism, the word has creative power. Every prayer pronounced sincerely is a weapon against evil, an instrument of alignment with the cosmos. Sraosha is the spirit ensuring this word is not lost. He conducts prayers to the divine plane, purifies sounds, translates the heart's murmur into language understandable by the immortals. Without him, words would be noise. With him, they become bridges.

In rituals, his invocation is constant. He is honored during night hours, moments of decision, vows of silence, initiation and farewell ceremonies. His function as soul protector also links him to funerary rites, where his presence is invoked so the spirit's passage occurs safely and clearly. He is the first called upon when discernment is desired. And the last to leave when the soul finds itself.

In the contemporary world, Sraosha remains a profound reference. In a time saturated with sounds, distractions, voices clamoring for attention, his figure invites retreat, inner listening, spiritual vigilance. He reminds that true spirituality lies not just in visible acts, but in what is heard in silence. In what is perceived when all else falls quiet. He teaches that consciousness is alive. That ethics is not an external code, but an inner voice. That the spiritual life begins when one listens more than speaks, observes more than judges. He is the bridge between knowing and being. Between hearing and acting. And every time a soul decides not to yield to anger, deceit, vanity—every time it chooses, even in silence, the juster path—Sraosha is there. Invisible. Present. Vigilant.

Contrary to what many might imagine, Sraosha's presence is not restricted to mystical spheres or ceremonial moments. He infiltrates everyday gestures, small silent decisions, moral dilemmas arising unannounced. His action reveals itself when someone chooses to listen to an uncomfortable thought instead of silencing it with distractions; when a difficult truth is welcomed instead of rejected. This inner listening, cultivated with discipline and sensitivity, is a field where Sraosha sows discernment and reaps clarity. In a world where speech is used to dominate, his presence rescues listening as an act of freedom and courage.

Therefore, his vigil should not be understood as control, but as support. He does not impose; he sustains. He does not dictate paths; he illuminates them from within. Consciousness, that intimate and non-transferable territory, finds in him a silent yet unshakeable ally. In the noise of our internal conflicts, his voice is almost always discreet—but it is precisely its delicacy that makes it unmistakable. When we move away from the tumult and approach what pulses authentically, it is Sraosha who accompanies us, offering not ready answers, but the possibility of formulating the right questions. And thus, he continues his office without fanfare, sustaining the flame burning in the core of every being seeking truth. Between shadows and lights, errors and learnings, he remains attentive, not as judge, but as presence. In the true listening that pierces words, the ethical choice made even without audience, the peace sprouting from wholeness-lived silence—it is there Sraosha reveals his face. Not as an end, but as a path always inviting continuation.

Chapter 22
Rashnu, the Weigher

When the soul leaves the body and approaches the Chinvat Bridge, where the definitive crossing separates the just from the wicked, it is Rashnu who positions himself at the center of judgment. His role is austere, precise, relentless. He is the spirit of absolute justice, the one who weighs the deeds of human life on his spiritual scales. And his scales know no favoritism, respond to no pleas, tilt for no emotion: they respond only to truth.

In Zoroastrianism, the judgment of the soul is not moral fiction or psychological metaphor—it is spiritual reality. Every thought, word, and action leaves a mark on the invisible fabric of being. The soul, upon leaving the body, carries these marks, which cannot be hidden. Rashnu, the Weigher, does not create these marks; he merely reveals them. He is the reflection of the life lived, unblemished objectivity, the eye seeing reality without veils.

The name Rashnu means, in essence, "the Just," "he who is straight." And righteousness here is not merely formal. It is internal coherence between what one thinks, says, and does. His function in the soul's tribunal is to balance the two pans of the scale: on one side, deeds of good; on the other, deeds of evil. But it is not cold accounting. What weighs is not just number, but intention, depth, impact. A sincere act of kindness, performed in a moment of great temptation, can weigh more than dozens of correct gestures done out of convenience.

Yet, Rashnu is not a solitary judge. He acts alongside Mithra, guardian of covenants, and Sraosha, spirit of awakened consciousness. While Sraosha protects the soul from deceptions and Mithra observes broken commitments, Rashnu calculates. His judgment is like a mirror: it does not condemn, merely reveals. And the soul, seeing itself reflected in this mirror, understands clearly whether it is worthy to cross or if it will fall.

Rashnu's scales are a central symbol in Zoroastrian spirituality. They are simultaneously ritual object, ethical archetype, and cosmic instrument. On the liturgical plane, they appear in symbolic representations of judgment. On the ethical plane, they are the standard of conduct. The faithful lives aware they will be weighed. And no weight can be hidden. Nothing escapes his gaze: neither disguised intentions, nor hidden acts, nor guilty silences.

Rashnu's justice is absolute, but not punitive. He does not condemn for pleasure. He neither rejoices in the wicked's fall nor is moved by the repentant's lament. He simply acts. His neutrality is his strength. His impartiality, his glory. For the just, his presence is liberating. For those who lived duplicitously, it is feared. He is the boundary between illusion and consequence. Between discourse and essence.

In Zoroastrian rituals, Rashnu is remembered in moments of moral reflection. His image evokes seriousness, sobriety, responsibility. He is invoked before important decisions, in reconciliation ceremonies, in prayers for justice in times of social injustice. His presence inspires righteousness as a lifestyle. He teaches that justice is not revenge, nor mere external balance—it is order within the being.

In the spiritual body of the universe, Rashnu acts as the weight preventing creation's collapse. Good must have real weight. Justice cannot be a vague ideal—it needs to be measurable. Every time a human being acts truthfully, their action is not lost. It falls onto the scales. And its weight contributes to keeping the Chinvat Bridge possible. With every lie, betrayal, act of cruelty, the scales tilt, and the bridge narrows.

But Rashnu also holds a lesson of mercy. Because his justice is not automatic. He recognizes change. True repentance has weight. Rectifying an error is worth more than maintaining the error. What he demands is sincerity. What he evaluates is the heart's direction. And even if someone has strayed, if their last steps were firm on the path of truth, they may be sustained.

The scales, in this sense, are also an invitation. They serve not only to weigh the dead—they serve to guide the living. Every faithful who remembers Rashnu in their choices weighs their words before speaking, measures their actions before acting. Lives with balance. And this balance is not passivity: it is strength. It is the firm center amidst the world's pressures.

In Zoroastrian tradition, those living under Rashnu's gaze are the freest. For they know truth ultimately prevails. That justice does not sleep. That everything will be revealed. And that the correct life needs no witnesses—only integrity.

Living under Rashnu's constant presence is walking with an acute sense of consequence, not out of fear of punishment, but from the intimate understanding that every gesture shapes destiny. He offers no shortcuts, accepts no masks, nor bows to self-pity. In times when truth is often distorted to serve interests, his figure rises as a symbol of lucidity and firmness. Rashnu reminds that life is a field of choices, and that, even amidst the world's uncertainties, there is an invisible order observing, recording, and one day revealing with precision what each being was in essence.

This spiritual clarity, however, does not nullify compassion. The justice Rashnu represents is not the negation of hope, but its truest condition. He does not close paths; rather, he shows which are truly open. The scales he carries, with their capacity to perceive the value of repentance, dignify the human effort to reverse evil, to seek good even after error. This makes Rashnu a guardian not only of judgment but of evolution. He weighs not just where someone has been, but where they are moving—and this inner movement is what can redeem even the most fragmented stories.

Rashnu's presence, therefore, is not a burden, but a constant reminder of the freedom dwelling in truth. Under his gaze, each life is measured justly, but also with an exactness recognizing the complexity of being human. In the end, his scales do not condemn, merely reflect. And reflecting oneself in them is perhaps the deepest experience of self-knowledge: the moment when the soul, stripped of illusions, finds its own measure—and with it, the real possibility of crossing the bridge.

Chapter 23
Atar, the Spirit of Fire

Among all elements revered in Zoroastrianism, fire is undoubtedly the most visible, symbolic, and sacred. But fire is not just a physical phenomenon—it is, above all, a spiritual presence. This presence has a name and consciousness: Atar, the sacred spirit of fire, living spark of truth, luminous witness of the covenant between the human and the divine. He is the flame that not only burns but reveals. The light that not only illuminates but purifies.

Atar is not a fire god, as conceived in other pantheons. He is a Yazata, a spirit created by Ahura Mazda to serve as one of the most direct intermediaries between the human and spiritual planes. His flame represents truth in its purest form, for fire consumes impurity, repels falsehood, reveals what is hidden. That is why Zoroastrian fire is never allowed to extinguish: it is not a simple symbol—it is a concrete manifestation of sacred presence.

In Zoroastrian temples, fire occupies the center. It burns on high altars, in sacred chambers where only the initiated may enter, where the flame is kept alive with dedication, care, and reverence. But this fire is not just fuel—it is spiritual energy. It is present in every prayer, offering, purification. Every significant Zoroastrian ceremony happens before the fire. The flame is witness. It sees, hears, remembers.

The name "Atar" also carries, at its core, the idea of essence. He is more than physical fire: he is inner fire, the fire of the awakened mind, clean consciousness, true word. When a faithful speaks truth, it is said Atar ignites in their voice. When someone acts righteously, Atar shines in their gestures. When inner darkness is fought, Atar consumes the residues of falsehood. He is, therefore, a spirit both external and internal—flame and inner flame.

In older traditions, Atar is described as a resplendent young warrior, bearer of clarity, fighter of falsehood. He is the direct enemy of Angra Mainyu and his servants, for lies cannot stand before light. He acts in silence, like all profound truth. His presence is felt, more than seen. But when he manifests, everything transforms: the false is revealed, the impure burned, the true exalted.

Fire is also a bridge between worlds. In funerary rituals, Atar's fire is kept burning to guide the soul in the darkness of crossing. It illuminates the path to the Chinvat Bridge. It purifies thoughts, burns emotional residues, dispels fears. The soul that lived truthfully does not fear Atar—it recognizes him as an ally. But the soul that lied, betrayed, corrupted its own spark, fears his presence, knowing it can no longer hide.

Atar is also present in life's four fundamental elements: he is the sun's heat, wood's combustion, bodies' energy, the spark in the just one's eyes. He lives in homes, temples, sacred words. His maintenance is one of the noblest acts of Zoroastrian priesthood. Caring for fire is caring for truth. Feeding it is reinforcing order. And its extinction, voluntary or negligent, is considered a sign of spiritual disorder.

Among Zoroastrian homes, it is customary to keep a small flame or lamp lit during important moments—birth, marriage, prayers, seasonal celebrations. This domestic fire is an extension of the temple fire. One need not be a priest to honor Atar. Every faithful can be guardian of the flame, provided they do so with reverence, purity, truth. For Atar does not dwell where there is falsehood. His presence demands integrity.

He is also the spirit of applied justice. In judgments, disputes, ethical decisions, Atar is invoked as light of clarity. He does not decide, but illuminates. Does not interfere, but reveals. Before his flame, deceptions dissipate. It is no coincidence that it's said every true oath must be made before fire. For he listens. He records. He responds.

And there is, still, the inner fire—the fire each human being carries in the core of their consciousness. Atar burns within the just. It is he who warms the faithful's heart, illuminates discernment, consumes inner shadows. Cultivating this inner flame is an essential part of the spiritual journey. Without it, no righteousness endures. Without it, darkness spreads. But with it, even the smallest truth becomes light enough to guide the soul amidst chaos.

Atar's presence, thus, transcends ritual space and touches the deepest layers of being. He is not just invoked—he is cultivated. In every ethical gesture, sincerely spoken word, thought seeking truth over convenience, Atar's spark strengthens. Fire, far from being a static symbol, becomes inner movement, constant transformation. It ignites the illusory and warms the integral, reminding that the purification process is continuous and requires constant vigilance. The spirit of fire not only illuminates the world—it demands it be awake.

Those treading the path of righteousness recognize that carrying Atar in the heart means accepting truth's presence as an uncompromising companion. There is no room for half-words, nor ambiguous intentions. The inner flame cries for authenticity. In daily life, this reflects in silent choices, invisible ethical confrontations, moments when conscience prevails over desire. And when the world becomes opaque, Atar presents himself as the one clearing vision—not offering ready answers, but making permanence in falsehood impossible. He reveals the moral landscape in all its sharpness, without adornments or shadows, and this clarity, though sometimes painful, is also liberating.

In the end, Atar remains as watchman and companion. He demands not grand sacrifices, but constancy. Demands not fear, but sincerity. He is the living presence transforming homes into sanctuaries, words into commitments, and lives into testimonies. Carrying his flame is accepting that truth burns, but does not consume—it forges. And that the guiding fire is the same that purifies, welcomes, reminds: wherever true light exists, there Atar will be, firm, silent, burning with the serene intensity of all that is essential.

Chapter 24
Haoma, the Divine Plant

At the ritual heart of Zoroastrianism, where matter meets spirit and offering becomes a link between human and divine, there is a sacred plant not just consumed, but revered: Haoma. It is not just vegetation—it is spirit. Not just drink—it is presence. Haoma is both plant and divinity, body and being. And its sap nourishes not only the body: it strengthens the soul, purifies the heart, illuminates thought.

In Zoroastrian tradition, Haoma occupies a central place in the Yasna rituals, where it is prepared, consecrated, and ingested as part of communion with the sacred. Its preparation is not simple: involving grinding green branches, mixing with pure water, and reciting specific prayers during the process. It is not just any potion. It is a vivified drink, a vegetal essence turned spiritual vehicle. When consumed, it not only nourishes—it transforms.

But Haoma is not just a plant in the botanical sense. He is a living spirit, a conscious entity created by Ahura Mazda to offer vigor, longevity, and spiritual enlightenment. He is the spirit of plant life in its purest form, the principle of growth, renewal, and inner fortitude. In some traditions, Haoma is described as a celestial priest, a man of light, whose words heal, whose eyes see truth, whose body is medicine.

The etymology of the name "Haoma" suggests movement, extraction, transformation. He is, therefore, the spirit of spiritual alchemy: what is taken from earth, prepared consciously, and offered to the sacred becomes path to the divine. His sap symbolizes unbreakable vitality. No ritual of power lacks his presence. His presence invites integrity, courage, renewal.

The most revered Haoma is the golden one, described as a luminous plant, with a living aura, whose effects are not restricted to the physical body. According to Avesta hymns, past heroes—including Zarathustra himself—drank Haoma and thereby received spiritual strength, clear vision, protection against evil. He is not drug. Not escape. He is awakening. Intensified presence.

On the liturgical plane, Haoma is prepared with extreme reverence. Priests handling it must be in a state of purity, with righteous thoughts and clean intentions. During the Yasna, the drink is offered in chants, dialogues with creation spirits, as if Haoma himself were present, listening, responding, strengthening. Its ingestion is limited to specific moments, because it is not utilitarian consumption, but an act of communion.

Haoma is also a symbol of spiritual longevity. In his hymns, he is praised as "he who wards off death," "he who heals the sick," "he who strengthens the just." He promises not physical immortality—but spiritual vitality that does not corrupt. Drinking it consciously, the faithful is not just strengthened: they are aligned with truth. It is as if the plant's sap flows through the soul's channels, dissolving lies, healing wounds, rekindling the inner spark.

He is also protector of mothers and children. Tradition associates him with fertility, gestation, safe childbirth. Offering Haoma to pregnant women was a gesture of blessing, connection with life in formation. His energy is both masculine and feminine. He fertilizes, but also welcomes. Gives strength, but also heals. He is not polarized—he is total. Reflects nature's own cycle, where birth and death are parts of the same dance.

In Zoroastrian mythology, Haoma is also a combatant of evil. His light repels *daevas*, his sap purifies spiritually corrupted spaces. In spiritual battles, his presence is invoked as shield. Not by brute force, but intense purity. Evil, for Zoroastrianism, cannot withstand the presence of what is essentially pure. And Haoma is liquid purity, the incorruptible vegetal spirit.

In symbolic representations, Haoma sometimes appears as a luminous tree, other times as a radiant figure with a chalice in hand. These images, far from idolatry, are pedagogical manifestations of his function: reminding that life is on earth, but its origin is celestial. Reminding that the body is temple, and that every food, if consecrated, can be sacrament. Reminding that even what grows in silence carries within it the strength of a divinity.

In the contemporary world, although the specific original plant of Haoma is not identified with certainty—with hypotheses ranging from ephedra, rue, and others—his spirit remains active. Rituals with

Haoma continue among Parsis and other Zoroastrians. His symbolic ingestion, liturgical memory, sacred chant still echo. He is one of the last living links between body and the most concrete spirituality. A divinity allowing itself to be touched, prepared, shared.

Haoma is, thus, more than plant. He is path. He mirrors humanity's spiritual condition. Teaches that, even coming from earth, it is possible to become vehicle of light. That, even in vegetal body, it is possible to contain wisdom. That, even being harvested, prepared, consumed, his essence remains alive—for it is not the plant's body that is sacred, but its consciousness.

Haoma's presence in Zoroastrian tradition reveals a profound teaching about the interconnection between nature and spirit, ritual gesture and inner transformation. Drinking Haoma, one ingests not just a substance—one performs a silent pact of renewal and listening. He reminds that life is a current flowing between planes, and that even what sprouts from earth carries a luminous origin. In his vegetal simplicity resides a spiritual potency traversing times, bodies, worlds, offering the faithful not instant miracle, but the possibility of transmuting existence through alignment with truth.

Haoma teaches there is wisdom in the slow rhythm of growth, in attentive listening to what blossoms without fanfare. He invites an embodied spirituality, not denying body or matter, but transforming them into channels of the sacred. His careful preparation, specific prayers, ritualized ingestion—all point to a different relationship with the world: one of reverence, presence, listening. He is the reminder that what nourishes the body can also nourish the soul, if harvested respectfully, consecrated intentionally, received gratefully. And that this union between vegetal and spiritual is not exception—it is model.

In the end, Haoma remains a living link between visible and invisible, sap and consciousness. His mystery lies not in being fully understood, but in being experienced wholly. He guards, in every drop, the possibility of reconnection: with earth, light, oneself. As spirit, he continues circulating where there is sincere search for clarity and vitality. And in every faithful opening to this communion—whether in temple, chant, or inner silence—Haoma is reborn. Not as plant, but as living presence of what is pure, essential, and incorruptible.

Chapter 25
Fravashis, the Protectors

In Zoroastrianism, where every force in the universe is endowed with consciousness, and every element of the world participates in a moral and spiritual order, there exist entities that transcend the boundaries between the visible and invisible worlds. They are not truly born, nor do they die. They exist between the eternal and the transitory, the individual and the collective. They are the Fravashis—the invisible protectors, the immortal essences that accompany, inspire, and defend human beings, the elements of nature, and even the heroes of the past. They are not just ancestral spirits—they are the purest reflections of being.

The term "Fravashi" carries a complexity that cannot be reduced to a single definition. In its origin, the word points to the "higher self," the "eternal essence," the part of the being in direct connection with the cosmic order. Each person possesses their Fravashi—an ideal, immortal form that precedes birth and survives death, observing and accompanying the soul's earthly journey. This essence is not a copy, but a spiritual matrix, a spark of the divine project each human being carries within.

The Fravashis are not restricted to the living. They also include ancestors—those who lived in justice, righteousness, fidelity to the light. Heroes who defended truth, sages who taught wisdom, parents who lived with dignity—all continue to live through their Fravashis. These spirits, though not central worship figures in Zoroastrian cult, are constantly invoked and honored. Not as gods, but as guardians, companions on the journey.

There are also Fravashis not linked to humans. There are Fravashis of mountains, rivers, ancient trees, protective animals. The entire creation, in its most essential form, possesses this spiritual double anchoring it in order. When praying for nature's protection, one is often asking for the Fravashis of mountains and waters to intervene. To care, inspire, restore balance.

During the Farvardigan festivals—days dedicated to the dead and ancestors—the Fravashis receive symbolic offerings: fire, water, flowers, simple foods. It is believed they visit the living during this period, walk among houses, listen to prayers, gather longings, restore hope. It is a time of communion between worlds. There is no fear of death among Zoroastrians who know the Fravashis—for they know death is merely transition, and the link with their own never truly breaks.

The primary function of the Fravashis is protection. They protect against evil's assaults, spiritual deceptions, moral weakness. They are always present in moments of doubt, inner conflicts, difficult choices. They do not speak in an audible voice—but their presence is felt like a breath of clarity, a silent reminder of who one is. Many ancient accounts tell of people saved by a sudden impulse, an inexplicable intuition—understood as manifestations of the Fravashis, acting silently to preserve the just path.

There is also the dimension that Fravashis inspire. They are not just shields—they are beacons. They illuminate the path the soul must tread to align with its highest form. What a person could be, in their fullest state of righteousness and consciousness, already exists as a Fravashi. And life is the continuous effort to become worthy of this essence. That is why evil cannot touch anyone's Fravashi—it is inviolable. And even if the soul errs, strays, becomes corrupted, the Fravashi remains intact, waiting, inspiring, guiding.

Zoroastrianism teaches that, upon dying, the soul meets its Fravashi again. And this reunion is decisive. The soul, looking at its own essence, understands all it was, all it could have been, and all it still can be. If it lived in consonance with this higher spark, it is welcomed. If not, it is invited to reparation. But judgment is not punishment—it is revelation. And the Fravashi is witness and light.

In sacred texts, Fravashis are described as beings of light, firm as rocks, pure as Atar's fire, silent as Sraosha, immortal as Ameretat. They are forces that do not impose, but sustain. When a soul succumbs to despair and finds strength to rise, it is the Fravashi lifting it. When a difficult decision is made with courage and clarity, it is the Fravashi that inspired. They do not act in the soul's place, but show the way. They are the living reminder of what is possible when one chooses good.

In daily life, remembering the Fravashis is maintaining a constant connection with the ideal. It is living as if having a spiritual mirror observing. Not out of fear, but respect. Love. Because one knows there is something more, something greater, something eternal watching us—not to judge, but to guide. And this something is not outside, but within. It is part of one's own being.

Honoring the Fravashis is honoring the lineage of light. It is recognizing one does not walk alone. That there is a chain of wisdom and justice preceding us, enveloping us, impelling us. And that, one day, we too will be Fravashis for those to come. That our choices today will echo in descendants' consciousness. That our light, if cultivated, will serve as a beacon for other souls in other eras.

The consciousness of living under the silent gaze of the Fravashis transforms every gesture into seed and every choice into legacy. They do not impose, but sustain; do not interfere, but point—with a firm delicacy present when all seems to crumble. In this bond, there is a spiritual pedagogy: Fravashis not only protect, but teach. Teach to be integral even in anonymity, act righteously even without guarantees, remember that each step can be light for someone yet to come. In the invisible weaving of existence, they keep the fabric cohesive, linking past, present, future by a golden thread that never breaks.

More than ancestor worship, the relationship with the Fravashis is recognition of the eternity dwelling in the instant. When one acts courageously, chooses good despite cost, insists on truth amidst noise—it is the Fravashi becoming active, vibrant, mirroring within the being the image of the soul in its fullness. They are not just projections of the human ideal; they are the living memory of everyone's divine origin. And that is why, even in the darkest moments, even when all seems lost, there is always a spark insisting on burning. This spark is the Fravashi's promise: that there is still a path, still meaning, still light.

Living up to one's own Fravashi is the silent challenge permeating the earthly journey. And upon understanding it, the faithful no longer walks alone, but in alliance with something transcending them. It is not about perfection, but direction. A subtle, constant commitment to the best version of oneself—the one already existing, already observing, already waiting. And when, one day, the soul finally reunites with this presence that was always there, it will recognize not just who it was, but who it never ceased to be. For the Fravashis are not ghosts of the past, but seeds of the eternal in each of us.

Chapter 26
Duality in Spiritual Beings

In the intricate spiritual tapestry of Zoroastrianism, where each entity carries a purpose and a well-defined identity, emerges a more subtle and, at times, disconcerting layer: the presence of duality in certain spiritual beings. Although the Zoroastrian worldview establishes a clear contrast between the forces of good, commanded by Ahura Mazda, and those of evil, originating from Angra Mainyu, there are entities whose nature seems to oscillate, reflect ambiguities, or even mirror, in reverse, an antagonistic counterpart. This chapter delves into these figures inhabiting the thresholds—neither entirely light, nor purely shadow.

The essence of Zoroastrianism is clear moral opposition: Spenta Mainyu, the Benevolent Spirit, and Angra Mainyu, the Destructive Spirit, represent two realities that coexist but never merge. However, among the Yazatas and other spiritual beings, this absolute clarity is sometimes shrouded in layers of tension. Some entities, though fundamentally benevolent, manifest aspects or attributes that can resemble opposing forces. Others are mirror doubles, whose functions become more understandable when examined in light of their opposite.

There are, for example, Yazatas presenting behaviors or domains requiring interpretive vigilance. Mithra, the guardian of covenants, whose function is to ensure justice and adherence to truth, is also a spirit who watches incessantly, demands flawless fidelity, punishes those breaking alliances. His brilliance can be as relentless as the sun itself, and in his figure lies the danger of light that burns when misused. Justice without compassion, truth without measure, can become shadows—and it is there duality insinuates itself as warning.

Sraosha, the spirit of listening and obedience, is another example of perceived ambiguity. His power is silent, nocturnal, intimate. He watches thoughts, accompanies the dead, protects the living during sleep. But this contact with the world of the dead, with the inner shadows of the human mind, gives him proximity to the threshold between light and darkness. It is precisely this constant crossing that makes him strong. Sraosha does not fear darkness—he illuminates it from within. But his nature reminds that spiritual vigilance is not only done in daylight, and that even purity must know darkness to overcome it.

Besides these dubious aspects within the Yazatas themselves, Zoroastrianism also recognizes the existence of evil equivalents, the so-called *daevas* or *drujs*. These spirits of falsehood, confusion, chaos, and death often represent the direct inversion of an entity of good. Just as there is Asha Vahishta, the Supreme Truth, there is *Druj*, the spirit of falsehood, who seduces with appearances of truth and corrupts order. Like a shadow imitating light's form, *Druj* is Asha's distorted reflection.

This mirror structure reveals a complex spiritual reality: evil, in Zoroastrianism, does not create—it corrupts. Angra Mainyu lacks Ahura Mazda's creative power. His forces manifest through distorting what already exists. That is why many *daevas* seem like grotesque imitations of Yazatas. Their strength lies in lies, appearance, deceit. They possess no true essence— only parasitize energy diverted from the original order.

There are also entities possessing similar names or functions, but whose interpretation varies by context. An example is the Fravashis. Though essentially protective and associated with light, records exist where their energy, when neglected or forgotten, becomes unstable, disturbing. This does not mean Fravashis become evil, but rather that, as conscious spiritual forces, they demand recognition and alignment. Inadequate invocation, lack of honor, can generate imbalance—and in this imbalance, arises the disequilibrium resembling evil.

This idea of duality as an invitation to responsibility is central. Good is neither static nor automatic. It needs cultivation, invocation, maintenance. The absence of spiritual upkeep opens space for imbalance's infiltration. Thus, evil is not an autonomous, creative force—it results from choices, forgetfulness, deviations. Even essentially good entities, if misunderstood or poorly related to, can become sources of fear or confusion.

Duality, therefore, is not relativism. Zoroastrianism does not dissolve the boundary between good and evil—on the contrary, it sharpens it. But it recognizes evil arises not as a separate being: it infiltrates as corruption, distortion, shadow cast by misdirected light. Zoroastrian spirituality, at this point, is profoundly ethical: the world's order depends on constant moral choice, active vigilance, conscious alignment with truth.

This vigilance is also expressed in rituals. Every Zoroastrian ceremony carries specific formulas to ward off *daevas*, purify spaces, maintain focus on good. It is not superstition—it is responsibility. The awareness that evil acts in failures, negligences, the soul's gray areas. Where there is no clear presence of light, shadow settles. And therefore, every Yazata, even the kindest, demands attention, invocation, connection.

Duality in spiritual beings reveals, therefore, that the world is not made of absolute, immutable figures. It is made of relationships. It is in how the human being relates to these forces that their nature reveals itself. The same spirit can protect or disturb, depending on the inner alignment of the invoker. The guiding light can blind. Healing water can drown. Purifying fire can consume.

This relational understanding of Zoroastrian spirituality shifts focus from the ontology of entities to the ethics of contact. Spiritual beings, though having intrinsic natures, manifest with greater or lesser intensity according to the individual's inner disposition and moral posture when invoking or ignoring them. Spirituality ceases to be just a belief system and becomes a field of living interaction, where human responsibility is permanent and non-transferable. Thus, duality resides not properly in the entities, but in the channels through which they express themselves—and these channels are always human, sensitive to intention, zeal, truth.

This means evil, however threatening, always depends on the weakening of good. Imbalance arises not as frontal attack, but silent hollowing, a crack through which falsehood insinuates itself. In Zoroastrianism, the spiritual battle is won not just with faith, but constancy, subtle vigilance, the continuous commitment to sustain good even in simplest gestures.

Ambiguous entities like Sraosha or Mithra are not paradoxes, but reminders that spiritual complexity demands maturity. They reflect the human challenge itself of sustaining light in a world where everything can be inverted, where the just can become tyrannical if losing sense of measure. In this scenario, duality reveals itself as ethical lens, not theological contradiction. It educates the gaze, alerts the spirit, demands discernment. Teaches that spiritual power is not neutral: it responds to how it is activated. Therefore, understanding the dubious nature of certain beings does not weaken Zoroastrianism's moral clarity—on the contrary, it strengthens it, by demonstrating the struggle between good and evil inevitably passes through the field of consciousness. And it is in this awakened consciousness, capable of invoking purely and resisting firmly, that the spirit's true victory rests.

Chapter 27
Invocation Rituals

In Zoroastrian spirituality, the relationship with spiritual beings—Ahura Mazda, the Amesha Spentas, Yazatas, Fravashis—is not merely contemplative. It is active, alive, deeply ritualistic. Zoroastrianism does not view the divine as a distant entity, to be merely understood or worshiped in thought, but as a real, summonable presence, which can and should be invoked to align the human soul with cosmic order. And it is in invocation rituals that this connection becomes tangible, when word becomes bridge and gesture, vehicle of light.

Zoroastrian rituals are not mere repetitions. They are recreations of the cosmos in miniature. Every detail, formula, instrument has a precise role. The invocation of spiritual entities is not done generically or symbolically: each being is called by specific names, detailed attributes, greeted according to function, involved in the network of relations linking invisible to visible. Ritual is a sacred language, carefully preserved, transforming ordinary time into sacred time.

The fundamental basis of these rituals is the word pronounced truthfully. Zoroastrian prayer is not improvised—it is chanted, intoned, vibrated. Texts from the Avesta, like the Yasna, Visperad, and Yashts, are recited with specific intonations, concentrated soul, purified body. The voice's sound, breath's rhythm, hymns' cadence—all participate in invocation. The word is spiritual seed: when cast into air, it germinates on the invisible plane. And the invoked being responds.

There are specific rituals for each category of spirit. The Amesha Spentas are invoked in larger celebrations, especially during the seven days of Farvardigan and during the Yasna, where each is called according to quality: Vohu Manah, the Good Mind; Asha Vahishta, the Supreme Truth; Khshathra Vairya, the Ideal Dominion; Spenta Armaiti, Loving Devotion; Haurvatat, Wholeness; Ameretat, Immortality. Each receives symbolic offerings: fire, water, foods, flowers—not as gifts, but recognition of their spheres of action.

Yazatas, in turn, are invoked according to specialties. Tishtrya, for example, is called in times of drought, with chants narrating his battle against the demon of sterility. Anahita is praised with prayers involving water, fertility, spiritual cleansing. Mithra is invoked to protect covenants, promises, agreements. Haoma is prepared and consecrated as liquid presence of the vegetal sacred. Each Yazata possesses own formulas, multiple names, sacred epithets. And the faithful invoking them must know, respect, call them reverently.

Purification is an essential step. Before any invocation, there are body and space cleansing rituals: ritual baths, white garments, preparation of sacred fire, use of tools like the *baresman*—a bundle of vegetal twigs representing connection with nature and spirits. The environment must be free of physical and spiritual impurities. For the Yazatas' presence cannot mix with corruption. They come when there is truth—and absent themselves when there is falsehood.

Fire, represented by Atar, is central in almost all invocation rituals. It is both offering and witness. The living flame, which must never extinguish during ritual, is kept burning as sign of Ahura Mazda's eternal light. It receives words, conducts them, purifies them. The rising smoke is the channel between worlds. The light kept burning signals truth remains alive. Fire is not object of worship, but the living altar where the invisible becomes presence.

In larger rituals, like the Yasna, priests—*mobeds*—perform specific roles. One recites, another responds, another prepares Haoma, another tends the fire. The ceremony can last hours. Each gesture is measured, each silence part of speech. There is no rush—there is sacredness. Ritual time is eternal time, where every second is filled with meaning. There, Ahura Mazda and his spiritual servants are called not as myths, but presences.

There are also domestic rituals, conducted by the faithful in their homes. The Zoroastrian home altar can be simple, but must contain essentials: a living flame, a vessel with pure water, fresh flowers, minimal food offerings. Prayers are recited in Avestan or consecrated translations. Invocation requires no intermediary when done truthfully. The faithful can, with purity and reverence, call Yazatas and Fravashis—and they will come.

Prayers are varied. Some are long chants, like the Gathas, attributed to Zarathustra himself, composed in poetic, philosophical language. Others are brief formulas, like Ashem Vohu and Yatha Ahu Vairyo, condensing entire Zoroastrian theology into few words. These verses are repeated throughout the day: upon waking, lighting fire, before meals, upon sleeping. Each repetition is a reminder: the sacred is not event—it is continuous state.

Invoking spiritual beings is not asking for favors. It is aligning oneself. It is declaring, with words and gestures, the desire to be on the side of order, truth, light. Zoroastrianism offers no easy promises. Yazatas do not grant whims. But they respond faithfully to fidelity. Their presence strengthens, purifies, guides. And ritual is the language of this alliance. A dialogue without disguises, a prayer that is more than word—it is choice.

These rituals, far from being religious ornaments, are spiritual anchors. They keep alive the flame of alliance between human and divine. They are practices shaping consciousness, purifying thought, leading the soul back to its center. And each time a faithful kneels before fire, recites sacred names, offers a flower, a chant, a silence full of truth—the world's order reaffirms itself.

This reaffirmation of order, however, is not mechanical or automatic act. It demands total presence from the practitioner—mental, emotional, corporal.

Invocation, in Zoroastrianism, works not like magic button, but as path of inner consecration. Pronouncing sacred names, performing gestures intentionally, the faithful not only calls spiritual beings: they transform themselves, they align. Zoroastrian ritualistics, therefore, is less about receiving external blessings and more about generating internal coherence. The sacred is not brought outside—it is awakened within.

This perspective reveals the demanding beauty of Zoroastrian worship: nothing is granted without consciousness. Faith, in this context, is less belief and more posture. It is the constant disposition to live in light's presence, even when the surrounding world seems shrouded in shadow. And rituals, with their discipline, symbolism, depth, function as maps for this spiritual crossing. They remind that contact with the divine depends not just on desire, but preparation—clarity of spirit, firmness of intention, righteousness of heart.

Therefore, invoking Yazatas, Amesha Spentas, or even Ahura Mazda, the Zoroastrian faithful not only performs devotional act, but participates in symbolic reconstruction of the universe. Each prayer, offering, lit flame is affirmation that the world can indeed remain in order—provided someone is willing to sustain that order truthfully. And thus, ritual ceases being just religious gesture to become, in its deepest sense, ethical commitment to light.

Chapter 28
Feminine Entities

In the vast spiritual pantheon of Zoroastrianism, where each entity manifests an aspect of creation and cosmic order, feminine figures are neither marginal nor secondary—they are central, essential, nurturing, and transformative. They do not merely represent the passive or receptive aspect of reality, as in many traditions relegating the feminine to a support function. In Zoroastrianism, the feminine is active force, spiritual consciousness, and moral foundation. Feminine entities not only coexist with masculine principles—they complement, balance, and sometimes guide them.

The first and highest among them is Spenta Armaiti, Loving Devotion, the embodiment of humility and earth. Her name already reveals her presence's nature: "Spenta" (beneficent, expansive) and "Armaiti" (piety, surrender, faithful love). She is not just abstract principle: she is concrete presence in the supporting earth, nourishing fields, soil welcoming bodies after death. She is the spiritual force of silent welcome and unconditional service. It is through her that creation remains firm and human beings learn to bow without debasing, serve without losing dignity.

Spenta Armaiti is also guardian of living faith. She demands not dogmas—she demands coherence. Her love is neither romantic nor abstract, but made of concrete gestures: care for earth, respect for food, silent gratitude for daily gifts. Her feminine is firm, maternal, inflexible in zeal for moral order. It is to her the faithful turns when wishing to purify themselves from arrogance, hardness, spiritual inattention. Her womb is the space where spirit reconciles with existence.

Another figure of immense power and reach is Anahita, the Lady of the Waters. She is more than a Yazata—she is a celestial queen. Linked to fertility, purity, protection of women, and spiritual fluidity, Anahita represents feminine power in its majestic form. She governs rivers, rains, births, hidden processes of gestation and renewal. Her presence was so powerful in Iranian tradition that many traits spread to other religions and cultures, celebrated even under different names but with the same essence.

Anahita does not merely protect—she combats. Her waters not only heal: they drown demons of impurity. Her dominion is not just sweetness: it is rigor. The feminine here is not synonymous with fragility, but uncontrollable potency, like overflowing rivers, cleansing tides. She demands purity, but also offers mercy. Those invoking her sincerely, even after error, are welcomed. Those using her as amulet without devotion are not recognized. Anahita sees the innermost—and responds to inner truth.

There is also a more hidden, yet hugely spiritually important figure: Daena, personification of moral consciousness and spiritual vision. Her name means "vision" or "inner perspective." She is described as a beautiful woman approaching the soul after death, assuming a form corresponding to the life lived: beautiful and radiant for the just, dark and deformed for those who lived falsely. She is the mirror of being. Truth reflected in feminine form. And it is with her the soul encounters before crossing the Chinvat Bridge.

Daena is not an entity that can be deceived. She is created by the soul itself throughout life. Every true thought, just gesture, righteous word shapes her beauty. Every deviation, lie, cruelty harms her form. She is the inevitable companion—the mirror following the spirit to the end. Not as punishment, but revelation. And it is her hand extending in the crossing to guide, or her absence making the path impossible to tread.

These three entities—Armaiti, Anahita, Daena—form a triangle of feminine spiritual strength. Armaiti sustains, Anahita purifies, Daena reveals. Together, they show the feminine in Zoroastrianism is not passive or decorative attribute: it is spiritual matrix of the real. They are forces modeling consciousness, body, destiny. They represent the depth of welcome, fury of cleansing, clarity of truth. They are aspects of creation, but also of salvation.

The cult of feminine entities in Zoroastrianism is discreet, but essential. There are no exclusive temples to them, but symbolic spaces where their presence is more intense: running waters, cultivated fields, altars where fire and water meet. Women, praying, giving birth, caring for the dead, become living channels of these entities. Men, honoring them, recognize the feminine not as other, but part. And invoking them, all faithful access a force transcending genders: the force of life bending without yielding, surrendering without getting lost.

These entities also reflect deep archetypes. Armaiti is the silent mother watching seed beneath earth. Anahita is the warrior of waters protecting the vulnerable. Daena is the lover of truth becoming judge after death. They live not only in rites, but dreams, choices, ethical instincts. They are inner presences, mirrors of what each human being can be when in harmony with creation.

In current times, where the feminine has often been distorted, silenced, or marginalized, Zoroastrian tradition offers a profound model of reverence and integration. It is not about exalting the feminine in opposition to the masculine, but understanding it as active, structuring presence. Feminine entities demand not blind adoration—they demand alignment with truth. Require not sacrifice—require purity. And their reward is clarity, protection, inner strength.

In the daily silence of ethical actions, care for the world, attention to interiority, these feminine entities continue living and acting. They depend not on grand rituals or sumptuous ceremonies to manifest presence: their strength reveals itself in coherent attitudes, compassionate gestures, moments of deep sincerity. Armaiti, Anahita, Daena are invoked not just with words, but with the way of being in the world. Every time someone chooses humility over arrogance, purity over chaos, truth over illusion, these figures become present, like invisible threads linking human to sacred.

It is in this sense Zoroastrian feminine surpasses religious symbolism and penetrates the sphere of lived ethics. It offers a spiritual path where power does not oppose care, firmness coexists with surrender, justice intertwines with mercy. Feminine entities do not compete with masculine principles—they challenge them to grow, rise, become more compassionate. They are the awakening breath, purifying water, revealing mirror. And therefore, their presence remains vital in a world still seeking balance between strength and tenderness, reason and intuition.

Thus, the feminine in Zoroastrianism is not just memory of ancient wisdom, but current invitation to integrate spirit with life's truth. Recognizing these entities as living parts of spiritual experience, the faithful not only honors ancestral tradition—they commit to a more integral, lucid, just existence. And in this silent commitment, these eternal figures continue guiding humanity towards its most luminous essence.

Chapter 29
Living Religion

Between the ancient echoes of the Avesta's scriptures and the living embers on temple altars, beats a still vibrant heart: Zoroastrianism remains a living religion. Its spiritual entities, rituals, prayers, and moral worldview belong not only to the past—they continue to guide, illuminate, transform the lives of real communities. And it is in the daily lives of Parsis in India, Iranis in Iran, and faithful scattered around the world, that the Zoroastrian Spiritual Pantheon breathes, acts, responds.

This permanence does not occur without challenges. Zoroastrianism, one of the oldest monotheistic religions of humanity, does not today possess the same number of followers as major global traditions. Its practitioners, though resilient, live surrounded by intense religious plurality and modernizations demanding adaptation. Yet, in every home where the sacred flame is lit at dawn, in every seasonal festival where the Gathas are sung, in every child learning to recite the Ashem Vohu, the tradition renews itself with the same force as Ahura Mazda's first creative breath.

The presence of spiritual entities in this contemporary context is more than symbolic: they are an active part of the faithful's daily spiritual life. The Yazatas, for example, are not just remembered in sacred books—they are invoked in prayers, mentioned in feasts, recognized as forces operating in the world. Mithra remains a pillar of integrity in business and social relations. His role as protector of covenants has become even more relevant in times of broken contracts and volatile words. Reciting his name reaffirms the value of honor.

Anahita remains alive in every purification ritual. Her sacred waters, though often symbolic in urban contexts, maintain their power of regeneration and healing. In festivals and marriage ceremonies, invocations to her fertility and protective blessing over homes are common. Her sacred feminine is updated in women leading communities, preserving tradition with wisdom and firmness.

The Amesha Spentas, in turn, are not just theological concepts—they are living moral guides. Living with Vohu Manah is cultivating pure thoughts. Acting with Asha Vahishta is seeking truth amidst shadows. Serving with Spenta Armaiti is working with humility and reverence. Zoroastrian spirituality, by its very structure, is existential—it does not depend on clergy to be lived. Each faithful, acting consciously, already performs worship.

The sacred fire, representing Atar, remains the most visible symbol of this continuity. In active temples in Iran and India—like the temple of Yazd or the Atash

Behram in Mumbai—the flame never goes out. It is tended with zeal, fed with pure woods, revered as presence of the sacred. The faithful gathering silently before the fire worship it not as idol, but as direct channel of light between material world and spiritual reality. Sitting before the fire is, still today, an act of listening, a moment of alignment with inner truth.

Contemporaneity has also required adaptations. Many young Zoroastrians live in global metropolises, far from traditional worship centers. But even in these contexts, Zoroastrian principles find new forms of expression: community meetings, online celebrations of seasonal festivals, study of sacred texts in virtual groups, transmission of chants via digital platforms. The sacred Zoroastrian enters the 21st century without losing its soul.

The continuity of worship of spiritual entities also passes through teaching new generations. Zoroastrian families teach their children early the names of the Amesha Spentas, the principles of duality between order and chaos, the power of free will. In many homes, the Avesta is kept in prominent places. The Avestan language, though no longer spoken, is preserved in liturgies, as a sacred tongue linking present to eternal past.

In religious festivals, the spiritual pantheon gains colors, aromas, music, forms. In Nowruz, the Persian New Year, each element on the Haft-Seen table refers to spiritual principles—health, truth, patience, rebirth. Yazatas are remembered as guardians of natural cycles, protectors of renewal. In Farvardigan, ancestors'

Fravashis are honored with devotion. Homes are cleaned, prayers recited, improvised altars receive candles and flowers. It is the time when the living make space for the dead, when invisible and visible celebrate together.

And there are still those who, not born into Zoroastrian families, approach the tradition for its profound ethical worldview. They seek Zoroastrianism not for promise of salvation, but inner resonance with the idea that living with good thoughts, good words, good deeds is, in itself, path of spiritual transformation. Some convert, others just learn. In all, the spiritual pantheon continues to touch, inspire, move. Zoroastrianism needs no proselytism to grow—it flourishes where there is truth, light, commitment to righteousness.

And thus, its entities live not just in temples, but in every choice made ethically, every gesture of care for creation, every decision taken with heart turned towards cosmic order. The Zoroastrian religion, therefore, lives because it is livable. It demands neither thoughtless sacrifices, nor blind faith, nor opaque dogmas. It invites consciousness, discernment, responsibility. And its spiritual entities, instead of remaining enclosed in the past, descend into the present with the same force they always acted: as companions, guides, protectors.

This vitality emanating from Zoroastrianism reveals a religious model not content with memory, but insisting on presence. The sacred, here, is not relic—it is everyday relief, living body breathing in ethical decisions and relationship with the world. The flame unextinguished in temples also burns inside those guided by justice, righteousness, clarity of spirit. And it is precisely this experiential dimension, independent of numbers, institutional recognition, or cultural hegemony, that guarantees Zoroastrian religion a continuity unbowed by time, reinventing itself within it.

What is preserved, then, is not just a set of symbols or narratives, but a way of being in the world affirming good as active choice. In a global scenario of moral uncertainties and spiritual disorientations, Zoroastrianism offers a path centered on responsible freedom—a path where the human being is called to be co-author of cosmic order. Yazatas and Amesha Spentas, more than distant entities, are faces of virtue in action, archetypes inviting the faithful to reflect, decide, act lucidly. They are also bridges between interior and exterior, eternal and present. It is in this continuous dynamic between tradition and transformation that religion stays alive. Because as long as there is someone who, upon waking, remembers to act with good thoughts; as long as there is someone who, facing fire or doubt, opts for truth; as long as there is a child learning a sacred chant with eyes lit by enchantment—Zoroastrianism will continue pulsing. Not as echo of glorious past, but living force still inspiring the world to be better.

Chapter 30
Philosophical Reflection

There comes a moment in the Zoroastrian faithful's journey—after study, practice, constant experience of rites and prayers—when the mind quiets and the spirit turns inward. Not seeking new external answers, but listening to the inner echo of truths already revealed. In that instant, each spiritual entity ceases being just figure, name, function, or power. They become living archetypes, dimensions of the soul itself, mirrors of the inner journey. The Spiritual Pantheon of Zoroastrianism, then, reveals its deepest face: that of a symbolic map of the human soul in its quest for light.

Each entity studied throughout this work can now be understood not just as an external spiritual being, but as an internal guide—a facet of one's own being on the journey of self-discovery, purification, elevation. Zoroastrianism, far from being just an exogenous theology, reveals itself as a spiritual philosophy offering the individual a moral compass and archetypal structure for soul growth.

Ahura Mazda, the Supreme Intelligence, is the original light shining within each awakened consciousness. He is not just a God who created the world—He is the principle of wisdom dwelling in the core of the just mind. He is the "higher self" calling the soul to live according to truth, compassion, order. Reflecting on Ahura Mazda is recognizing there is a divine spark guiding us not by imposition, but inspiration.

Angra Mainyu, in turn, is not just an external spirit of evil. He represents the potential for self-sabotage, the force of the corrupted ego, fear, lies, pride, inertia. He acts in daily choices where we opt to ignore good in favor of the easier, more convenient, more illusory. Defeating him is not destroying a being, but freeing oneself from his internal influences.

The Amesha Spentas are more than cosmic helpers—they are spiritual qualities each soul must cultivate. Vohu Manah, the Good Mind, represents the capacity to think clearly, compassionately, honestly. He is the discernment preceding every good action. Asha Vahishta, the Supreme Truth, is the inner axis of justice and righteousness. She is the ability to align with reality without distortions. Khshathra Vairya is the inner power ruling justly and courageously, not tyrannically. He is the strength to remain firm in good. Spenta Armaiti is humility and devotion, silent surrender to higher truth. Haurvatat, Wholeness, is the integration of soul aspects, emotional and spiritual health. Ameretat, Immortality, is the sense of eternity dwelling in the awakened soul—what does not die because it never ceased being aligned with Good.

The Yazatas, in their multiplicity, reflect the most dynamic aspects of spiritual experience. Mithra, judge of covenants, is the consciousness watching over our words' integrity. He is the commitment we make to our own evolution. Anahita, the purifier, is the capacity to wash ourselves of emotional stains, restart lightly. Tishtrya, bringing rains, is the potential for renewal the soul carries—faith that even in arid times, spiritual fertility can return. Sraosha, guardian of listening, is the archetype of inner silence—the part of us listening to the soul's call, remaining awake even when the world sleeps. Rashnu, the weigher, is our sense of inner justice, weighing acts not with guilt, but lucidity. Atar, the fire, is the fire of consciousness, transformation, awakening. Burns the false, warms the true. He is the "inner fire" every mystic recognizes. Haoma, the divine plant, symbolizes spiritual nourishment—what heals, strengthens, renews. In his inner dimension, he represents assimilated wisdom: the living word nourishing, truth transforming into strength. Fravashis, the protectors, are reflections of our higher self, spiritual ancestors dwelling in collective consciousness. They are our own best possible futures, already realized in light, calling us from beyond time.

And finally, entities like Daena, consciousness revealed after death, show Zoroastrianism understands the spiritual journey as integral process. Everything one is, does, thinks, shapes inner reality. There is no separation between spiritual world and practical life. Heaven and hell are experiences resulting from the quality of being. Judgment is not external, but internal—the soul reveals itself to itself, and that suffices.

This philosophical perspective of the Zoroastrian pantheon invites us to a new posture: disciple of one's own spirit. Each name studied, entity invoked, rite performed was, in fact, a stage in the journey of self-knowledge. Invoking sacred names activates inner qualities. Honoring Yazatas recognizes forces within us awaiting expression. Religion, then, becomes initiatory path, cosmology becomes spiritual psychology, myths become living metaphors of the soul.

Zoroastrianism, in origin, proposed not just theology, but a philosophy of living truthfully. The battle between Ahura Mazda and Angra Mainyu happens in the world, yes—but begins in each human soul. The Chinvat Bridge lies in every ethical choice. Rashnu's scales move with every thought. And Sraosha's listening activates whenever we silence the ego to hear light.

This is the depth of the Zoroastrian pantheon: it is not a polytheistic system worshiping multiple gods, but a multidimensional spiritual code, where each being represents a virtue, energy, part of the Whole. It is a living structure, usable as meditation map, ethics basis, guide for existential decisions. And the more the faithful internalizes these entities, the closer they approach their own luminous essence.

This internalization of the pantheon is not just philosophical abstraction, but concrete experience for those treading the path of consciousness. As each entity is recognized as living aspect of one's own being, spirituality ceases depending on intermediations and transforms into radical intimacy with truth. The faithful no longer walks seeking salvation as something distant but awakens to perceive salvation as continuous process of alignment with what is highest within. Religion, then, becomes presence—not structure followed out of fear, but horizon inhabited with lucidity and love.

This experience of the sacred as inner experience does not exclude the world but includes it in another key: ethical action illuminated by introspection. What was previously seen as external ritual gains symbolic and practical power as conscious gesture. Lighting fire, purifying with water, intoning chants—all are re-signified when done understanding each external act reflects internal disposition. Zoroastrianism thus reveals its profoundly initiatory character: each stage of its cosmology invites crossing ego layers, until reaching the being's luminous center, where Ahura Mazda's spark remains intact. At this journey's point, there is no need to separate religion, philosophy, psychology: everything converges to the same source. The faithful arriving here does not merely believe—they know, because they live. And in this living, understands good is not distant ideal, but daily choice. That entities are not beyond, but within. That judgment will not come, because it is already happening. And that the soul, mirroring itself in this archetypal pantheon, discovers what it always was: light in motion, inseparable part of the Whole.

Chapter 31
Unity in Diversity

Upon reaching the apex of Zoroastrian spiritual contemplation, one comprehends a truth transcending the pantheon's complexity, the rituals' richness, the names' multiplicity: there is, at the heart of all forms, a single light. This light is Ahura Mazda, origin and destiny of all that is good, true, ordered. And although He manifests in myriads of beings—Amesha Spentas, Yazatas, Fravashis, spiritual archetypes, feminine and masculine entities—all these are not fragmentations of a whole, but expressions of full unity. The spiritual diversity of Zoroastrianism is, in essence, a hymn to creation's unity.

Each spiritual entity, as revealed throughout the journey, fulfills a precise function within the great cosmic body. But none acts isolatedly. Like organs of a living organism, they intertwine, communicate, complete each other. Vohu Manah prepares the mind to welcome Asha Vahishta's truth. Spenta Armaiti welcomes in the heart what Khshathra Vairya organizes in just action. Haurvatat and Ameretat, together, restore the soul's integrity and eternity, forming a pair announcing life's fullness.

Yazatas, in turn, are like the universe's sensitive nerves. Each responds to a field of creation. But all obey the same principle: keeping the world cohesive, beautiful, functional. They do not compete, overlap, claim glory. Their glory is serving Ahura Mazda's order. They prove that, even in multiplicity, it is possible to live in perfect harmony. And this harmony reflects primordial order, the order existing before time, creation, and continuing when the world is renewed.

Zoroastrianism, by sustaining this unity through diversity, presents a profoundly inclusive conception of the sacred. It is not about gathering names by accumulation. It is about understanding each name is a face of Truth. Each spiritual being represents an access route to the real. There is no hierarchy among them in the human sense of power, but rather functional organization revealing each part's value in the whole. What sustains the sky is not just sunlight, but also stars' firmness. What maintains earth is not just mountains' solidity, but also waters' flow.

This vision also reflects in human life. The individual, living with good thoughts, words, actions, acts as microcosm of this greater harmony. They become, by choice and practice, reflection of cosmic order. And each person, regardless of social position, family role, knowledge level, possesses a spark of this unifying light. Ahura Mazda dwells equally in all, manifesting fully in those firmly choosing good.

Rituals, names, offerings, chants—all these instruments, though precious, are not ends in themselves. They are means. Portals. Languages. The true destiny of the Zoroastrian soul is not just performing rites perfectly, but aligning with the unique light giving meaning to all practices. And this light manifests in daily actions: kindness to neighbor, honesty in business, compassion for animals, reverence for nature.

Zoroastrianism also invites contemplation of this unity beyond religious limits. It is, in essence, a theology of conscious choice. Every soul is free to adhere to good or evil, light or shadow. And this freedom proves Ahura Mazda's trust in His creation. If evil still exists, it is not because good is fragile, but because freedom is real. And it is in this freedom each soul reveals its most divine face: by incessantly choosing light.

The multiplicity of entities also teaches the sacred can manifest in many forms. In a star, flame, plant, gesture of silence. He who has eyes to see and ears to hear will recognize everything—absolutely everything—can become connection path to the eternal. There is no place Ahura Mazda is not. No form that, purified, cannot reveal His presence.

At the end of all invocations, studies, meditations, the Zoroastrian faithful understands spiritual entities are, ultimately, emanations of Ahura Mazda's absolute love and infinite wisdom. None acts independently. None separates from origin. And therefore, worship of them is also worship of the One. Plurality, far from dividing, reveals the richness of what is one. Light, passing through crystal, reveals multiple colors—but remains single light.

This wisdom also serves as bridge between traditions. The Spiritual Pantheon of Zoroastrianism presents itself not as exclusive truth, but deeply universal symbolic structure. Anyone living righteously, seeking truth, cultivating good, even without knowing Yazatas' names or reciting Avesta hymns, is somehow in communion with this light. Ethics, consciousness, compassion—these are languages everyone understands. And Zoroastrianism, in its deepest root, speaks them all.

Therefore, ending this journey is not closing a book—it is opening a path. Knowledge of the Zoroastrian Spiritual Pantheon is not end, but beginning. An invitation to internalization, daily practice, contemplation of beauty present in ordered diversity. May each name studied here not remain written word, but become living force in the reader's soul. May each entity become journey companion, inner master, star in the spirit's sky. And if each entity is a star, may the firmament built throughout this crossing remain visible even on existence's cloudy days.

The unity revealed in Zoroastrianism's spiritual diversity does not dissolve differences—it honors them. Teaches multiplicity is the One's language, and creation's beauty lies precisely in its complex harmony. There is no isolated virtue, solitary path, salvation that is merely individual. Everything pulses in relation, intertwining, synchrony. And it is in this living network of connections the human being discovers themselves active part of cosmic order—not spectator, but co-author.

Thus, knowing the Spiritual Pantheon is much more than learning about sacred entities. It is learning to look at the world with eyes of reverence, perceive sacred in everyday, recognize every true form of goodness is extension of Ahura Mazda's light. No just gesture fails to resonate in the universe's fabric. No sincere prayer fails to find echo. The profound teaching of this unity is that, even facing apparent chaos, there is silent order operating—and the faithful, choosing good, reinforces, expands, manifests it. This is, finally, Zoroastrianism's living heritage: a call to lucidity, responsible freedom, communion with the luminous principle sustaining everything. The pantheon, with all its symbolic richness, is not labyrinth to be deciphered, but multifaceted mirror reflecting the spirit's journey towards wholeness. And may this journey continue, now, within each reader—silent, firm, luminous—like the flame that never goes out.

Epilogue

There comes a moment, after the last page, when silence gains density. Not the silence of absence, but of deep presence. It is in this instant that knowledge ceases to be reading and becomes revelation. And what has been revealed in this journey is more than an ancient worldview—it is a spiritual mirror returning to human beings the forgotten responsibility of being a conscious link between the visible and the invisible.

What pulses in this book does not belong only to the past. It is a living call. A reminder that, behind the history of Zoroastrianism, behind the names and rituals, there exists an architecture of reality that remains active. The battle between light and shadow is not limited to cosmic myths or celestial characters. It is present in every choice, every thought born in the human mind, every seemingly small gesture that silently tilts the destiny of an entire world.

Throughout these pages, it became impossible to ignore the magnitude of free will. The revelation that we are not at the mercy of blind forces, nor angry gods, but inhabit a morally structured universe, where each being is co-creator of order or accomplice of chaos. There is no neutrality. Reality does not accept passivity. And it is precisely this ethical lucidity that makes the spiritual journey presented here so transformative.

Good is not a comfort—it is a task. Truth is not a belief—it is a stance. Spirituality, as we learned from Zarathustra's words, is defined not by repeated dogmas, but by actions aligned with cosmic order. Living righteously is, in Zoroastrianism, the highest act of faith. And this demands vigilance, clarity, courage.

At the end of this reading, it is possible to perceive the purpose was not to present a closed system of beliefs, but to open space for consciousness to breathe again. The Amesha Spentas are not mythical characters—they are living archetypes within us, aspects of universal wisdom dwelling in our own being. The Good Mind, Supreme Truth, Loving Devotion, Wholeness, Immortality... each of these emanations is also an invitation to inner integration. They point the way back to the center—a center found not in distant temples, but in the intimacy of the spirit itself.

Nor can one emerge unscathed from the confrontation with Angra Mainyu—the principle of destruction. Not as a distant entity, but as a recurring whisper in our indecisions, inner lies, tendency to postpone good for convenience. The book presents him not as a caricature of evil, but as a symbiotic reality that can only be faced with non-negotiable integrity. By recognizing this adversary, we also recognize our strength. For every shadow only reveals its weakness before a light refusing to extinguish itself.

And this light—this inner fire—is the greatest heritage of this spiritual legacy. Not a fire to consume, but to purify. A fire lit in consciousness and maintained by coherence between thought, word, and action. Ahura Mazda's fire needs no external altars; it lives where there is truth, compassion, silent firmness before what is just. It does not burn to be worshiped, but to remind that divine presence is clarity, direction, living wisdom.

At this point in the journey, the reader leaves not just informed—but transformed. For seeds planted here will continue germinating in the invisible spaces of daily life. Perhaps in a moment of doubt, perhaps facing a difficult choice, perhaps in a simple gesture of care for the earth, for another, for oneself. The true Zoroastrian rite is not in temples, but in attention to life as sacred. There is no separation between the spiritual and the mundane when one learns to see with the eyes of the awakened soul.

Ending this reading is, in fact, beginning a new cycle. A cycle where knowledge converts into posture, faith transforms into action, the sacred incarnates in routine. The bridge has been crossed—and now it is impossible to return to the same starting point. Because whoever understands the greatness of choice no longer allows themselves to live on autopilot. Revelation, once received, cannot be forgotten without consequence.

You now carry with you more than information: you carry a call. A call to lucidity, righteousness, active construction of a world where good is not exception, but foundation. There is no predicting how this will manifest in your personal journey. But one thing is certain: the seed has been planted. And, like everything truly sacred, it will know how to blossom at the right time.

May the light that burned in these pages continue burning within you. May the silence remaining after reading be fertile. And may the flame of consciousness—this living temple unbent by time—never extinguish.

www.ingramcontent.com/pod-product-compliance
Lightning Source LLC
LaVergne TN
LVHW040056080526
838202LV00045B/3662